Also by Rich Landau and Kate Jacoby

Horizons: The Cookbook

Horizons: New Vegan Cuisine

Rich Landau & Kate Jacoby

Foreword by Joe Yonan

vedge

100 Plates

Large and Small

That Redefine

Vegetable Cooking

THE EXPERIMENT

NEW YORK

VEDGE: *100 Plates Large and Small That Redefine Vegetable Cooking*
Copyright © 2013 Rich Landau and Kate Jacoby
Foreword copyright © 2013 Joe Yonan
Cover, interior, and author photographs copyright © 2013 Michael Spain-Smith

The Experiment, LLC
220 East 23rd Street • Suite 301
New York, NY 10010-4674
www.theexperimentpublishing.com

Many of the designations used by manufacturers and sellers to distinguish their products are claimed as trademarks. Where those designations appear in this book and The Experiment was aware of a trademark claim, the designations have been capitalized.

The Experiment's books are available at special discounts when purchased in bulk for premiums and sales promotions as well as for fundraising or educational use. For details, contact us at info@theexperimentpublishing.com.

Library of Congress Cataloging-in-Publication Data

Landau, Rich, 1967-
  Vedge : 100 plates, large and small, that place vegetables in the
spotlight / Rich Landau and Kate Jacoby.
      pages cm
  Includes index.
  ISBN 978-1-61519-085-0 (cloth) -- ISBN 978-1-61519-177-2 (ebook)
  1. Cooking (Vegetables) 2. Cooking (Fruit) 3. Vegan cooking. 4.
Vedge (Restaurant : Philadelphia, Pa.) I. Jacoby, Kate, 1980- II. Title.
  TX801.L297 2013
  641.6'5--dc23
                                        2013012098

ISBN 978-1-61519-085-0
Ebook ISBN 978-1-61519-177-2

Cover design by Susi Oberhelman
Text design by Pauline Neuwirth, Neuwirth & Associates, Inc.

Manufactured in the United States of America
Distributed by Workman Publishing Company, Inc.
Distributed simultaneously in Canada by Thomas Allen and Son Ltd.

First printing August 2013
10 9 8 7 6 5 4 3

Our son Rio Jacoby-Landau
is a self-proclaimed
vegetarian. He travels
with us and never fails
to impress us with his
approach to food and
capacity for joy.
This book is for him.

contents

soups and stews

the dirt list

desserts and baked goods

foreword

MY FRIEND DANIEL is scraping clean a plate of salt-roasted golden beets. Actually, three of us are all clinking forks, battling like musketeers for the last bites of this terrine-style dish, in which the beets are layered amid chunks of smoked tofu and avocado. The flavors and textures seem so made for one another that they must be part of some traditional dish, but of course they aren't. Rich Landau has married them.

"How does he do it?" Daniel mutters, to himself as much as to anyone else.

That pretty much sums up the vibe at my table whenever I've eaten at Vedge, my favorite restaurant in Philly. People make involuntary noises of approval midbite; they push plates around with a spoon as they try to get those last few droplets of sauce; they close their eyes as they swallow, then open them and chuckle out loud; they make exclamations and proclamations, ask questions and fumble for answers.

Our server calls Rich a "magic man," but his brand of prestidigitation isn't categorically different from the creative, difficult work that any great chef undertakes to transform ingredients into beautiful, satisfying, sometimes even exciting dishes. Except, of course, for the fact that Rich isn't using every trick in the book. By avoiding all animal products, he challenges himself to think of the purest way to express the character of his favorite vegetables, while still making food that appeals

even to the omnivores in the room, of which there are plenty. But these aren't dishes that rely on mock-this or faux-that sleights of hand. It's not that kind of magic. The result of Rich's legerdemain are plates on which the starring ingredients' natural flavors shine, where sparks of heat or salt or spice work as punctuation but aren't the ultimate point. The ultimate point is the showcased flavor of something that was recently pulled from the dirt.

I'm not the only one who enjoys bringing carnivores to Vedge, in a sort of "Can you believe it's vegan?" game. It's just too much fun to see the same kinds of reactions as the ones I had the first time I ate there. When I ate that meal, I wasn't quite ready to declare myself a vegetarian but I was finding myself drawn ever more exclusively to vegetables. Simultaneously, I was skeptical of vegetarian and vegan restaurants, because, like so many people, I had eaten far too many mushy veggie burgers and tempeh "chilis" and sandwiches on leaden bread overstuffed with sprouts. Even the upscale places often disappointed me, as if they held themselves to an altogether different (that is, lower) standard from that of the omnivorous ones.

At Vedge, Rich and Kate Jacoby (his wife, co-owner, and pastry-chef magician in her own right) have created a restaurant that feels absolutely of the moment, with a menu that features everything most of the people I know enjoy eating. That means small plates, designed for sharing. Lots of fermented, charred, pickled, and smoked foods. Global spice blends—many of them plenty spicy—from the world's boldest cuisines: Korean, Southeast Asian, Japanese, Turkish, American Southern. A drinks list full of the finest spirits in perfectly balanced cocktails infused with fresh herbs and spices. A sophisticated yet approachable wine list. And a staff able to walk that delicate line between efficient and friendly, so knowledgeable about the restaurant—so clearly happy to be part of it—that they infect every customer with enthusiasm, too.

They call it a vegetable restaurant, not a vegetarian or vegan one, and only once you eat there do you truly understand that distinction. Rich's dishes are jubilant celebrations of vegetables, not an attempt to accommodate a so-called dietary restriction.

I said that Vedge is my favorite restaurant in Philly, and that's true. It's a strong enough statement, given that the city is home to such standouts as Vetri and Zahav and their sister restaurants, not to mention the many smaller chef-driven places that are equally committed to quality. But the truth is, it's one of my favorite restaurants on the East Coast, and in the country, really. I'd put it up against anybody's. Not that I have to, of course. Because despite the comparisons, Rich and Kate are happy doing what they're doing: drawing people to Center City Philadelphia to taste the magic for themselves.

Now that they've spilled some of their secrets in this book, of course, you'd think that I might be a little more reluctant to make the train trip from DC to Philly. You'd be wrong. It's true that I'll be cooking my way through this book, and have started already. I can't wait to learn how Rich gets that *dashi* stock so flavorful without using any dried tuna flakes, or how he manages to make hearts of palm seem so comfortable atop curried lentils. But by the time I do, he will have no doubt picked up another bag of tricks, and there will be only one way to experience them. I'll happily be back on that train.

JOE YONAN is the two-time James Beard Award–winning Food and Travel editor of *The Washington Post* and the author of *Eat Your Vegetables: Bold Recipes for the Single Cook* (Ten Speed Press). He is also the author of *Serve Yourself: Nightly Adventures in Cooking for One*, which Serious Eats called "a truly thoughtful, useful, and incredibly delicious book." He was a food writer and Travel section editor at *The Boston Globe* before moving to Washington in 2006 to edit the *Post's* Food section, for which he also writes the Weeknight Vegetarian column and occasional feature stories. His work from the *Globe* and *Post* has appeared in three editions of the *Best Food Writing* anthology. Joe spent 2012 in North Berwick, Maine, on leave from the *Post* to learn about growing and homesteading from his sister and brother-in-law.

introduction

A SENSE OF time and place.

A reporter recently asked me why vegetables are so "in" right now, and that is how I responded. More than anything else, it's the vegetables that define our culinary seasonality. If there are ramps in your pasta and some asparagus on your plate, it must be early May. If you're grilling zucchini, I'm guessing you're in flip flops in the late summer. And I'm betting by the time you're buying apples and acorn squash, you're probably dusting off some Halloween decorations. The world has become smaller for many of us, but there remains a growing season that cycles back each year. The farm to table movement we're cheering for these days is nothing new, but it does wake up our common food consciousness. We're spending more time learning about what we're eating and where it's coming from, and vegetables are wonderful teachers.

So Vedge is a vegetable restaurant. We put vegetables front and center on our plates, celebrating the huge range of different flavors, colors and textures that the plant-based world gives us throughout the year. From signature dishes to the ever-evolving Dirt List, from our Cocktail List to our Desserts, we hope to give the world more examples of just how inspiring and satisfying vegetables can be.

I remember loving vegetables as early as kindergarten when a guest came in to do a cooking demonstration for our class. Boiled baby carrots in salt water—it didn't matter, I was

hungry. But in their simple state—not covered up with spices or cloaked with sauce—these carrots transcended food and became a delicious expression of pure garden freshness. I still remember vividly how that carrot tasted.

Then on *Sesame Street* one day I saw something that really caught my eye. "Mrs. Wilson's garden" was a campy 60's video (you can find it on YouTube) of a girl who went to visit a woman named Mrs. Wilson in her country home. There they pulled up vegetables from the garden, cooked them and ate them right there. Corn, tomatoes, carrots, beets. So fresh and so clean. These visions of what vegetables were supposed to be (versus what I was served for school lunches) just blew my mind and stuck with me forever.

Years later when I decided that eating animals was an ethical issue for me I turned to vegetables for my diet and never looked back. Oh sure I ate mock meats, lived on pizza and hoagies for a while and of course I have never been perfect. A plant-based diet is a state of mind, an approach to food—it's not a club, cult or religion. Go ahead, call us vegans if you want—it's good enough for Bill Clinton, after all—but although Vedge uses no animal products whatsoever in its kitchen, we prefer to stick with the title that refers to the food, not the diet. *We are a vegetable restaurant.*

Farm to table may be in vogue, but vegetables have always come from farms, which is why I was one of the first to join the chorus of chefs who find it hard to keep a straight face sometimes when promoting this concept. And I'll admit that when I see the big box food people start to boast it in commercials it's hard not to roll my eyes.

Vegetables have always grown in the ground. And while the rest of the world's food culture has been living eating seasonally and "farm to table" uninterrupted for centuries, we have all of a sudden decided that this is some new great concept of ours.

Oh we Americans have strayed far indeed… we are guilty of eating fresh tomatoes in December and of buying processed foods and supporting mass agro businesses. We have been doing it for years and now we are getting fat and sick. So back to the farmers market we go, treating it like we invented it.

So it's easy for me to see both sides of this argument here. I am proud of us. Our obsession with food trends is overshadowed only by our obsession with diets. In the last 40 years we have gone from Lo-cal to Local and in-between we have gone carb free, fat free, salt free & gluten free. But look where we have landed: local seasonal produce that comes from farms—and gardens like Mrs. Wilson's. A diet and fad all-in-one; it's one that I hope will stick around. It should; it was here in the first place.

We have finally come home and realized that Americans are good at something we thought unlikely years ago… Food.

This is a great time to eat in this country. We are indeed waking up and I salute our "farm to table" mentality even if it is an old idea reborn.

■   ■   ■

On a recent trip to Jamaica, we consumed our "to do" list of local foods. Calaloo, cho cho, ackee, vegetable patties, jerk tofu, curry roti, breadfruit.

All this "exotic" food grows on the island, local indeed without the bumper sticker in sight promoting it. And now that we are getting back to this concept back home, how great is it that folks from other countries can visit us and have a great culinary memory to take away? Think that the USA is all fast food? We are happy to be one of the restaurants that proves that pre-conceived notion wrong.

This book won't bombard you with gory images and disturbing statistics. That has never been our approach and there are plenty of great books out there that can do that for you if you want. We are chefs, not activists. We love food, we live for food and we hope our passion for what we do passes through the pages of this book to inspire you to cook with a new sense of appreciation for vegetables. No membership or initiation to get in—just a desire to make yourself and your world healthier. What we're hoping for is that, little by little, the American culinary landscape will continue to celebrate the plant-based side of things. More than a passing trend, vegetables will continue to move from the peripheral side dishes to the centerpieces of our tables.

Vedge has been an extraordinary force in our life. We have connected with such diverse and fascinating people through it, from our wonderful staff to the customers who seem to have come in from everywhere to experience what they have heard about Vedge. What a singular honor, to be able to share what we love to do with so many people.

There are those who have followed us across four Horizons locations over eighteen years and two cookbooks, and we thank you for that. We couldn't have gotten to Vedge without you and we are so glad that you have embraced this concept of putting vegetables at the forefront of our dishes.

Then there are those who come into Vedge with a raised eyebrow (perhaps planning on getting a cheesesteak after their meal) who leave satisfied, shaking my hand and laughing at themselves for thinking that a meal of all vegetables couldn't be as satisfying as a meal with meat. But then there are those who are moved more profoundly, like the guy who ate two Big Macs for lunch one day, then dined with us for dinner, chose to go vegan, and never looked back. There are many of these stories, and before we go to sleep at night we think about them. And we drift off content, feeling nothing but gratitude that we have been able to take this journey.

In this book you will find a wide variety of recipes inspired by trips we have taken, ingredients discovered over the years, and a general desire to let the ingredients speak. Some preparations are quick and simple for the busy lives we all lead these days and others are more elaborate for celebrations or big family dinners at home. No recipes are intended to show off or intimidate. This is a cookbook, and in it are things that you will actually want to and be able to cook. As in the restaurant, recipes and headnotes for the Basics through the Plates (a.k.a. Mains) chapters are written by Rich, and Kate covers those in the Desserts and Baked Goods and Cocktails chapters. Our hope is that these recipes will introduce you to new ingredients while opening your eyes to new uses for vegetables you already know.

reading and preparing recipes

THESE RECIPES COME straight from the menu at Vedge, with the addition of other dishes we prepare at home ourselves and variations on dishes we think work well at home. Mirroring our departments at Vedge, all of the savory recipes are from Rich, and the pastries and cocktails are from Kate.

Each recipe was carefully tested to achieve the best results in a home kitchen. We provide a sense of how much time each recipe should take to prepare and to cook, and we give an idea of how many servings each recipe yields. The introductions to each recipe give you a little insight into our inspiration or some helpful information about ingredients. Most recipes double or triple very nicely.

At Vedge we are lucky enough to work with some of the freshest ingredients available—many of them unique. We offer tips about their seasonality and availability, and substitutions where applicable.

Remember, read the recipe ingredients and instructions through before you start your prep, and taste as you go to learn how the dish is coming together. People always eat first with their eyes, so take care to make your plates look beautiful. You'll see some suggestions for plating in our photography, but be creative in your own kitchen, and enjoy!

pantry essentials

I LIKE TO imagine that everyone reading this book will end up incorporating significantly more vegetables into their home cooking routines. For those readers who are completely new to 100 percent plant-based ingredients, there are a few items worth mentioning that are, in our opinion, no-brainer substitutions. If you buy the right brands, you get high-quality, clean products (made of pure ingredients, free from excessive process) that taste as good as or better than their animal counterparts. And regardless of "how vegan" your diet might lean, these will probably become your go-to brands of choice.

ACID

Acid from citrus juice or vinegar provides the high notes that bring life to your dishes. You also get this spike of flavor from other ingredients such as wine or mustard. Like salt, acid can also do a bit of "cooking," and it helps prevent oxidation. And like oils, certain acids can be more neutral on the palate (lemon juice or white vinegar), while others will clearly work better in specific recipes (preserved lemon or balsamic vinegar).

My favorite acidic note is sherry vinegar. Where many chefs add salt when they think a dish needs a wake-up, I add a tiny splash of sherry vinegar. Sherry vinegar is one of those mouth-watering, addictive ingredients that I would never try to

go without. Balsamic vinegar is also a great acid that carries a touch of sweetness. Balsamic vinegars vary greatly in quality, so I advise that you follow my dad's golden rule: "you get what you pay for."

CHILI PASTES

Spicy chili pastes and hot sauces have replaced ketchup on many of America's tables, and for good reason. A well-made chili sauce has a good amount of heat but also the right combination of flavors that make it multidimensional. Thai and Vietnamese chili pastes such as *sambal oelek* and sriracha have been mainstream for a while now, while Korean *gochujang* is just starting to catch on. Don't forget those humble New Orleans hot sauces either—they're still worth celebrating with!

ESSENTIAL CONDIMENTS

Worcestershire sauce is a unique combination of ingredients that you would never think of putting together, but at some point someone did, and this crazy complex brew was born. It's great for grilling and roasting vegetables (as long as it's mixed with a neutral oil). Our favorite brand of vegan Worcestershire sauce is Wizard's. We swear by it. Just read the ingredients, and you will find flavors from Asia, the Caribbean, and Europe, all mingling together to yield a sum greater than its parts.

You will have to search for vegan kimchi, and when you find it, stock up. It's already "spoiled" so it won't go bad if it's unopened. Try mixing ½ cup of kimchi in a food processor with 2 cups of vegan mayo and you will have an amazing new condiment that you will want to put on everything.

A good barbecue sauce is priceless. You can easily make your own by combining ½ cup of ketchup, 1 tablespoon of molasses, 2 tablespoons of agave nectar, 1 teaspoon of apple cider vinegar, and 1 tablespoon of a jerk, Latin, or Cajun spice blend.

HERBS

Once in a while, herbs are the central focus of a recipe (think pesto); most often, they are a last-minute addition

or finishing step. But that makes them seem secondary and unimportant. On the contrary, herbs are what make cooking interesting. Like spices, they are the punctuation marks to our cooking. Cauliflower with parsley screams Spain while cilantro takes it to Vietnam. On occasion, we call for dried herbs at the beginning of a soup or stew recipe, where they work best. Herbs can also speak of the seasons: lavender and basil in summer, rosemary and sage in fall. So use them as the powerful tools they are to convey what you want in your cooking. Buy them fresh and use them at the last minute in most of your recipes. Porcini powder is another great tool that has a richness to it that almost recalls chocolate. It will add depth to gravies and mushroom stock, and makes a great foundation for mushroom- and onion-based sauces.

MUSTARD

The range of mustards on the market today is staggeringly wide. You can buy the yellowest, brashest slop for a penny or the most expensive handcrafted whole-grain mustard, infused with truffles and wrapped in swaddling clothes! Seriously though, mustard is a great way to add zest and vitality to a dish, along with a bit of rich, creamy texture. If you buy only a single jar, go with a quality Dijon mustard.

OIL

A good cook knows when and how to use oil. Neutral oils with high smoke points are best suited for the early steps of cooking. Canola, grape-seed, safflower—these oils are ideal for roasting and searing. Richer-flavored oils like olive are better for adding texture and flavor to sauces and marinades that may or may not be exposed to some heat through cooking. When we call for olive oil in a recipe, we're always using a nice extra virgin olive oil. It doesn't have to be the most expensive one on the shelf, but it shouldn't be the cheapest either. Just make sure that you keep it fresh—buy small bottles and buy them frequently.

SALT

Salt enhances flavors. It also has the power to do some indirect cooking—curing olives, preserving lemons, brining tofu. There are times when sprinkling some coarse salt on the surface of a dish will add powerful flavor in a concentrated textural burst. Always buy sea salt. The quality is far superior to plain table salt, and it's the only thing we use in the restaurant and in these recipes. We also like to keep a smoked salt handy. Smoked salts are now widely available and can add that hint of campfire to a sauce or a surprising little sparkle to raw vegetables like radishes, carrots, or cucumbers.

TAMARI

Tamari is a Japanese soy sauce. And with soy sauce as with red wine, there is a wide range of quality. So splurge a little, and it will pay you back again and again. When you buy a bottle of soy sauce for $1.29 you are getting salt water (the equivalent of a wine you would drink out of a brown paper bag), but when you spend over $5 for a quality tamari you are getting a sophisticated brew that has body, richness, and a well-rounded mouth feel—not just salt. If you don't believe me, try them back to back.

TOFU

I'm often asked, "What kind of tofu should I buy?" At Vedge, we use only extra-firm tofu, but there is a remarkable range of tofu styles out there to explore. Japanese style is often silken tofu—delicious if done right, a disaster when done wrong. Its uses are very specific. The best way to introduce people to tofu is to buy a flavored tofu—smoked or five-spice tofu from an Asian market are good starting points. At Vedge, we use Fresh Tofu, a brand of artisanal firm tofu that has great texture. For the recipes in our book, we recommend using extra-firm-style tofu.

VEGAN BUTTER AND VEGAN SHORTENING

Butter adds flavor and structure to crusts, cakes, and custards. Shortening is less about flavor and more about building texture in things like crusts, dough, and cakes. We like the Earth Balance brand for their original vegan butter and vegan shortening, though their product line has expanded over the years with soy-free and coconut-based products as well. Feel free to use whatever brand you're comfortable with, keeping in mind that not all margarines are vegan (some contain milk proteins). And you'll definitely want to avoid any hydrogenated or partially hydrogenated oils.

VEGAN MAYO AND VEGAN SOUR CREAM

If we could make one quick change in every fridge across the country without anyone noticing, it would be the mayo. Follow Your Heart makes a fluffy, thick Original Vegenaise with a perfectly balanced tangy, creamy flavor. Best of all, its ingredient list is pure, simply substituting soy for eggs in the traditional mayonnaise recipe. This is one instance where we recommend this brand over its competitors. We use Tofutti brand vegan sour cream. They make a nonhydrogenated product that has fantastic flavor, texture, and color. It works beautifully wherever you might use traditional sour cream.

VEGAN MILK AND VEGAN CREAM

In most cases, we use soy milk, soy creamer, or coconut milk in our desserts based on their flavors and textures. We like Silk brand soy creamer as an alternative to whole milk or heavy cream. It's a touch sweeter, but the color and texture work well in baking. There is a plethora of plant-based milks available not just at natural foods stores, but at mainstream supermarkets and even discount buying outlets. If you want to experiment with them, almond and hazelnut milks are pretty close in texture to soy. Hemp milk has a distinctive flavor and is a little richer, more like coconut milk. Rice milk seems to be the leanest. Some plant milks also have very strong flavors, which can be desirable if they complement the theme of a dish.

WINE

White and red wine can be tremendously useful in the kitchen, adding flavorful high notes in the case of whites or rich flavors in the case of some reds. If you really want to get technical, lighter, dryer styles like Sauvignon Blanc or Grüner Veltliner will yield a pretty neutral acid to a dish. Viognier might add some floral aromatics, Gewürztraminer a touch of spice, Riesling some sweetness. Reds like Gamay can add some fruity tartness, Malbec might contribute a certain earthiness, and you'll gain extra richness and spice from the likes of Syrah or Cabernet Sauvignon. That said, unless you're following a recipe that is designed around a specific wine—for example, Madeira—don't worry too much about which white or which red you're using. Cooking the wine destroys some of the alcohol (depending on the cook time), but the overall nuances of flavor they provide are invaluable. When you have about a glass left of wine in a bottle, cork it and store it in the refrigerator for up to two weeks—this is the perfect wine to use for cooking. Or, better yet, open a new bottle to enjoy while you're cooking and use a little from that. Curious about whether your favorite wine is vegan? Vegan wines are not fined or filtered with any animal products. It's a common practice to use animal protein like egg white, gelatin, or isinglass to remove sediment from wines. These days, many winemakers are switching to plant-based options like clay or going the all-natural route and not fining or filtering at all.

basics

ANYONE CAN COOK. But *great* cooking happens when technique is applied to a strong foundation of flavor. In this section, we're arming you with some of our basics that serve as the foundation for many of our recipes and that you may also find useful for general cooking.

When it comes to stocks and spice blends, do what you feel comfortable with. There is no glory in trying to make stock from scratch if you don't have the time and it makes your life nuts. And likewise, there is no shame in having a vegetable bouillon cube around for the times when you just need to throw something together without a big production.

Same goes for spice blends. I love making our own spice blends at the restaurant because I can fine-tune them to the exact needs of the dish I am making. In the interest of full disclosure, at our house we keep a store-bought jerk and Cajun blend around. The recipes in this book are designed to make you happy and provide a sense of enjoyment. So whether you're a "from scratcher" or looking for some shortcuts, all of the end products will be delicious no matter what route you take to get there.

stocks

WITHOUT A WELL-MADE stock, no sauces or soups can come together properly. This is the foundation of good cooking.

At Vedge, our stocks change with the seasons. We do have a base of carrots, onions, celery, and leeks, but the other ingredients vary with what's on the menu and what's in season. In spring, the stockpot is full of asparagus bottoms, pea pods, outer leek leaves, and fennel fronds. In the colder weather, roots dominate the flavor of a heartier stock made up of trimmings from parsnips, turnips, and rutabaga, with perhaps some green cabbage leaves.

I wander around the kitchen during prep, greedily looking for odds and ends for tomorrow's stock. I scold those who throw away carrot tops and celery leaves, thinking they are trash. Shame on them; these trimmings are gold. This doesn't mean that dirty leek roots or beet greens belong in the stock. "The stockpot is not a garbage pail" was some of the soundest advice I ever got early on. To that, I also add "Don't throw anything in the stockpot that you wouldn't eat." (One exception: onion skin. It has a great flavor and it adds a golden hue to the stock.)

So, start saving those bits and pieces of vegetables in an air-tight container in your refrigerator until you have enough to make some good vegetable stock. Vegetable scraps will keep in the fridge for about a week. Homemade stock is economical, but don't get greedy; the vegetables can give only so much. The water line should just reach above the quantity of vegetable trimmings you have in your pot.

A nice trick we use at the restaurant is to brown the vegetables for extra flavor. Also, the vegetables should not be simmered forever (contrary to classic French technique). Some of the best vegetable stocks I've ever made were finished in under 30 minutes, all the flavors still bright and pronounced. So what are you waiting for? There's stock to be made!

vegetable stock

PREP TIME: 10 MINUTES

COOK TIME: 45 MINUTES

MAKES 5 QUARTS

2 teaspoons canola oil

6 carrots, chopped

3 stalks celery, chopped, preferably with leaves

2 leeks, rinsed well and chopped

2 onions, with skins, chopped

1 turnip, with skins, chopped

1 tablespoon salt

3 to 4 outer leaves of green cabbage

2 cups broccoli stems

2 cups kale stems

This all-purpose, all-season stock recipe works perfectly in any Vedge recipe. This will store for up to five days in the refrigerator. You don't need to peel any of the vegetables; just wash them carefully.

1. Heat the oil in a large stockpot over high heat until it starts to ripple. Add the carrots, celery, leeks, onions, and turnip. Cook, stirring, until brown, 3 to 5 minutes.

2. Add 6 quarts water and the salt and bring to a boil.

3. Reduce the heat to low, add the cabbage leaves, broccoli stems, and kale stems, and simmer for 25 minutes. Strain, cool, and store for use as needed.

Our mushroom stock is the base for many of our darker winter sauces and soups. It is also excellent enjoyed on its own as bouillon (broth) with fresh sliced enoki mushrooms. Keep leftover mushroom bases and stems in the refrigerator airtight for up to five days and remember to remove all dirt before getting started. This will keep for up to 3 days in the refrigerator.

1. Heat the oil in a large stockpot over high heat until it starts to ripple. Add the mushroom trimmings, onion, and dried shiitakes, and cook, stirring, until brown, 3 to 5 minutes.

2. Add 4 quarts water, the porcini powder, and the salt. Bring to a boil, then reduce the heat to low and simmer for 40 minutes.

3. Remove from the heat, stir in the rosemary, and steep for 5 minutes. Strain, cool, and store for use as needed.

mushroom stock

PREP TIME: 10 MINUTES

COOK TIME: 1 HOUR

MAKES 3 QUARTS

2 teaspoons canola oil

8 cups mushroom trimmings, wiped clean

1 onion, with skin, chopped

1 cup dried shiitakes

1 tablespoon porcini powder

3 teaspoons salt

2 rosemary sprigs

Dashi is the foundation of Japanese cuisine. We developed this version using seaweed (it must be *kombu*—no substitute will do) and dried shiitake mushrooms (instead of the traditional bonito, or powdered tuna). *Kombu* is available at Asian markets and natural food stores. Our shiitake *dashi* is my favorite stock of all—I often enjoy a cup of it on its own when it's finished. Stir in 2 tablespoons of miso paste (any type will do) for miso soup, or add greens and tofu for the best hot pot ever when you're feeling under the weather. It will keep for up to four days in the refrigerator.

1. Combine the shiitakes, tamari, kombu, and 4 quarts water in a large stockpot over high heat. Bring to a boil and simmer for 20 minutes.

2. Remove from the heat and let stand for 5 minutes.

3. Strain, cool, and store for use as needed.

shiitake *dashi*

PREP TIME: 5 MINUTES

COOK TIME: 35 MINUTES

MAKES 3 QUARTS

2 cups dried shiitakes

¼ cup tamari

2 ounces kombu seaweed

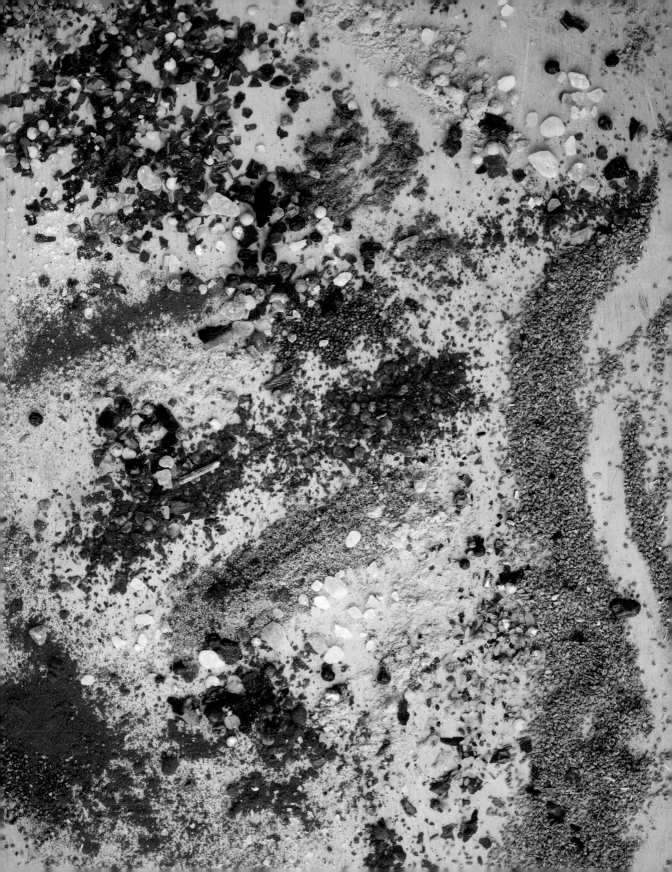

spice blends

SPICES ARE THE aromatic ingredients that build the flavor foundation in your cooking. Don't keep spices too long, or their potency will fade. Buy them in small containers, and don't be afraid to use them. Make sure to buy spice blends that do not rely on salt for flavor; if salt is the first ingredient listed, move on to another brand.

If you prefer to make your own spice blends, we've provided the recipes for some of our house blends that we call for throughout the book. These can easily be created at home in small batches working with small seeds and spices like caraway, coarse sea salt, peppercorns, and fennel seed. The beauty is that you can customize your blend to suit your own palate. Despise caraway? Leave it out. Love fennel? Add a bit more. But beware: once you get into the habit of making your own spice blends, you may develop a new addiction. Grind each spice individually to achieve uniform texture, then mix together. We recommend grinding each spice separately in a coffee bean grinder used only for spices; a mortar and pestle works well, too.

Spices should be very subtle on the palate. Use dashes here and there to add interesting dimension but never overpower. For instance, I love cumin, but I don't want to really taste it in my final dish. You should have to look for it. It should support and enhance the other ingredients, not dominate them. Like dried herbs, spices need to soak in or cook to dissipate their flavor.

montreal steak spice blend

2 tablespoons coarse sea salt

2 tablespoons black peppercorns

1 teaspoon caraway seeds

1 teaspoon coriander seeds

1 teaspoon cumin seeds

1 teaspoon fennel seed

1 teaspoon celery seeds

One at a time, grind each spice (except the celery seeds) in a clean coffee grinder or with a mortar and pestle to achieve a uniform consistency. Mix together, adding in the celery seeds.

island spice blend

1 tablespoon ground cumin

1 tablespoon granulated garlic

1 tablespoon granulated onion

1 tablespoon paprika

1 tablespoon salt

1 tablespoon freshly ground black pepper

2 teaspoons ground allspice

2 teaspoons brown sugar

2 teaspoons dried thyme

1 teaspoon ground ginger

1 teaspoon ground nutmeg

¼ teaspoon ground cloves

Mix all of the ingredients together.

latin spice blend

2 tablespoons paprika

1 tablespoon ground chile of your choice (such as chipotle, ancho, or cayenne)

1 tablespoon ground cumin

1 tablespoon granulated garlic

1 tablespoon granulated onion

1 tablespoon salt

1 tablespoon freshly ground black pepper

2 teaspoons dried oregano

2 teaspoons dried thyme

Mix all of the ingredients together.

Here are some other indispensable spices in our kitchen:

ALLSPICE: This dried berry will probably remind you more of a pumpkin pie or apple cider spice, but its origins are tropical. Almost all of the world's allspice is grown in Jamaica; in fact, it's sometimes called Jamaica pepper. Its sweet-spicy aroma is wonderful in an island-inspired curry. It is a necessity in jerk sauce, but use it sparingly; it can get overly pungent very quickly.

CUMIN: Cumin is earthy, nutty, and complex. Overdo it once, and you will hate it forever. For the best result, buy whole cumin seeds. When a recipe calls for ground cumin, toast a few in a pan over low heat until you just start to smell them, then grind them in a coffee mill or mortar and pestle.

FENNEL SEED: This powerful, licorice-flavored seed is a classic tomato-friendly accent. Use it whole or slightly crushed.

NUTMEG: Like allspice, nutmeg is another holiday spice with tropical origins—nearly all of the world's nutmeg comes from the tiny island of Grenada. In many places on the island, you can actually smell it in the air. With nutmeg and mace (the outer layer of the nutmeg), a little goes a long way.

SEAFOOD SEASONING: This aromatic blend of spices usually includes bay leaf and celery seed. There are plenty of brands available, but we stick by Old Bay.

SAFFRON: Saffron is the embodiment of the French and Spanish Riviera. This miracle flavor is expensive, but there is no substitute. Fortunately, most recipes call for just a tiny bit.

SMOKED PAPRIKA: This is one of my favorite secret weapons in the kitchen. It provides powerful, smoky flavors without the heat of chipotle. The flavor is entirely different from regular sweet paprika, so don't be tempted to make an even substitution.

WHITE PEPPER: The French love to use white pepper in cream sauces so that there are no black flecks, but to me, this spice is 100 percent Asian. A crucial component in Chinese five-spice powder, white pepper has a subtler flavor than black pepper.

small bites and small plates

IN THIS SECTION, we explore cocktail party bites, snacks, and small dishes to put out on your dinner table. These small bites take on different shapes and forms in different cuisines around the world—think of tapas in Spain or meze in Greece. They are ideal for entertaining when you don't have much time to cook. A few of these dishes, along with some wine and bread, make a surprisingly complete cocktail party. Many of these dishes keep for quite some time, so don't worry about making more than you need for one occasion.

At Vedge, we made the conscious decision to avoid listing many traditional salads on the menu. You will find a few in this book, but the majority of our cold plates are interesting preparations of vegetables, both cooked and raw, that are best enjoyed chilled or at room temperature. These cold dishes tend to be on the lighter side, their ingredients showcased with little textural or aromatic distraction. As a first course, they offer a refreshing way to work up the appetite and prepare the palate for the remainder of the meal.

charred *shishito* peppers with smoked salt

PREP TIME: 5 MINUTES

COOK TIME: 5 MINUTES

SERVES 4 TO 6

2 tablespoons canola oil

½ pound shishito peppers, with their stems

1 tablespoon smoked coarse salt

We like to refer to *shishitos* as the Japanese jalapeño. They have big flavor with a little bit of heat. They pack a punch even if you cook them thoroughly, but when you half-sear them, as in this dish, their full flavor really shines through. Charred *shishitos* are equally delicious at room temperature or right out of the fridge. If you can't find *shishitos*, try using Cubanelle peppers. Sear them for a little longer depending on how large they are.

1. Heat the oil in a large sauté pan over high heat until it ripples and nearly smokes.

2. Carefully add the peppers in a single layer, and allow them to sear in the hot oil for 1 minute, until the skins blister. Do not flip the peppers.

3. Transfer the peppers to a paper towel to absorb any excess oil.

4. If serving immediately, arrange the peppers in a serving dish and sprinkle with the salt. Alternatively, allow the peppers to cool at room temperature for 20 minutes before transferring them to an airtight storage container. Store in the refrigerator for up to 3 days. When ready to serve, transfer the peppers to a serving dish and sprinkle with the salt

olives

THE ALLURE OF olives goes far beyond a love of salty foods. The variety in their flavors and textures is nearly as wide as their geographic reach and cultural significance. Olives evoke a perfect Mediterranean day, perhaps in a vineyard in the Tuscan or Provençal countryside, or at a terraced cliffside café on a Greek island overlooking the silky blue Aegean. Our table there is set simply with bowls of olives, pistachios, bread, and olive oil—and, of course, some local white wine.

As unabashed olive lovers, we have spent countless hours foraging through specialty stores, making questionable deals with obscure purveyors, and scouring the Internet for the favorites that make up the mixes we serve at Vedge. Our green mix consists of green Cerignola, Castelvetrano, and Picholine olives. Our black mix consists of black Cerignola, Taggiasche, and cured Beldi olives. Here are some others worth seeking out:

green

GORDAL: Also known as the Spanish Queen, this giant olive is similar to the green Cerignola but a little less fruity.

HALKIDIKI: Commercially known as Mount Athos, this Greek olive gets stuffed with everything from garlic to sweet peppers to almonds. In its pure, unpitted form, it is salty and addictive.

LUCQUES: These seasonal prizes from France are best known for their bright garden-green crunch.

black

LECCINO: A briny black olive, Leccino is the Italian answer to French Niçoise and Greek Kalamata.

BOTIJA: This intensely sour purple Peruvian olive packs a punch—the Botija is for serious olive enthusiasts only.

BLACK MANZANILLA: Less common than its green counterpart, this medium-size Spanish olive has a crisp, juicy texture.

green olives with preserved lemon and fennel

PREP TIME: 5 MINUTES,
PLUS 30 MINUTES RESTING TIME
COOK TIME: 5 MINUTES
SERVES 4 TO 6

6 to 8 cups mixed green olives, drained

1 tablespoon chopped preserved lemon

1 tablespoon juice from preserved lemon

1 cup white vinegar

1 tablespoon sugar

2 teaspoons salt

1 fennel bulb, white parts only, thinly sliced

We like to highlight the herbal flavor of green olives with a shot of lemon and licorice-y fennel. At Vedge we use equal parts green Cerignola, Castelvetrano, and Picholine olives, but you could also try Lucques, Halkidiki, or Gordal. You can find preserved lemon at a gourmet market or online.

1. Toss the olives in a medium bowl with the preserved lemon and lemon juice. Set aside.

2. Combine the vinegar, sugar, and salt in a small saucepan. Bring to a boil over high heat, then add the fennel and cook for 3 minutes. Drain the fennel, reserving the liquid if desired (see Tip).

3. Add the fennel to the olives, toss again, then allow the mixture to sit at room temperature for at least 30 minutes before serving. This will keep for up to 2 weeks in the refrigerator.

tip: Use this basic brine for anything you want to pickle (cucumbers, green beans, carrots), then get creative and flavor the brine with crushed red pepper flakes or whole seeds—try mustard, caraway, dill, coriander, nigella, poppy, celery, fennel, or cumin. Experiment with different combinations and have fun! Just bring the brine to a boil and you are ready to go. Pour the hot brine over what you want to pickle, seal it up, and in 24 hours, you have pickles. If you are pickling roots such as beets or carrots, bring them to a boil in the brine (rather than just pouring the brine over them) and let them boil for about 3 to 5 minutes before sealing. This way they will be tender.

This is our house black olive recipe. We use a mixture of equal parts black Cerignola, cured Beldi, and Taggiasche olives, but you could substitute high-quality Kalamata, Leccino, or Botija. They get a nice little kick from the crushed red pepper flakes, which wake up the fruity flavors of the olives.

1. Toss the olives in a medium bowl with the reserved brine, jalapeño slices, and red pepper flakes.

2. Allow the mixture to sit at room temperature for at least 30 minutes before serving. This will keep for up to 2 weeks in the refrigerator.

black olives with fresh and dried chiles

PREP TIME: 5 MINUTES, PLUS 30 MINUTES RESTING TIME
SERVES 4 TO 6

6 to 8 cups mixed black olives, drained, ¼ cup brine reserved

½ cup seeded, finely sliced jalapeños

1 tablespoon crushed red pepper flakes

baby cucumbers with *sambal* and peanuts

PREP TIME: 15 MINUTES,
PLUS 20 MINUTES RESTING TIME
SERVES 4 TO 6

2 pounds Persian cucumbers, cut diagonally into ½-inch-thick slices

1 teaspoon salt

¼ cup sambal oelek

2 tablespoons sriracha

1 tablespoon toasted sesame oil

1 tablespoon tamari

2 teaspoons sugar

2 teaspoons Chinese black vinegar

1 cup roasted salted peanuts, chopped

2 tablespoons fresh cilantro leaves

This Southeast Asian–style cucumber salad is for heat seekers. Here, we build the depth of flavor with complex Chinese black vinegar and tamari, then add two chili sauces: sriracha and *sambal oelek*, its chunky Vietnamese cousin. Topped off with the powerful flavors of cilantro and peanuts, this is not just heat for heat's sake. The cucumbers can be served as an appetizer or side dish. If you can't find Persian cucumbers, substitute English cucumbers or even peeled and seeded standard cucumbers. Pick up a bottle of Chinese black vinegar at an Asian market; you'll be happy to have it for the Roasted Cauliflower recipe (page 90).

1. Toss the cucumbers with the salt in a large bowl.

2. Combine the sambal oelek, sriracha, sesame oil, tamari, sugar, and black vinegar in a small bowl. Add to the cucumbers and toss until all of the cucumber slices are coated evenly.

3. Let the cucumbers stand at room temperature for at least 20 minutes, but not more than 2 hours or they will begin to turn soggy.

4. Garnish with the peanuts and cilantro and serve.

daikon "summer rolls"

PREP TIME: 30 MINUTES,
PLUS 20 MINUTES RESTING TIME
SERVES 4 TO 6

¼ cup plus 2 teaspoons rice wine vinegar

1½ teaspoons salt

1 teaspoon sugar

2 large, thick daikon radishes (about 1 pound), peeled

1 tablespoon peanut oil

1 tablespoon sambal oelek (optional)

1 teaspoon freshly ground black pepper

12 ounces prebaked, Asian-marinated tofu, cut into thin strips (see Tip)

1 cup loosely packed fresh basil leaves, preferably Thai basil

1 cup peeled, julienned carrots

1 cup loosely packed fresh cilantro leaves

1 cup peeled, seeded, julienned cucumbers

½ cup chopped scallions, white and light green parts only

¼ cup seeded, thinly sliced jalapeños

The signature flavors of Vietnamese cuisine—acidic tinges of fresh lime, the powerful combination of basil, mint, and cilantro, and haunting lemongrass-infused tofu—resonate in this take on classic summer rolls. These rolls, which appeared on our opening menu at Vedge, aren't wrapped in a chewy rice paper wrapper, but rather with salted daikon sheets. Inside, the crunchy vegetables and tofu combine the best aspects of a summer roll and a tofu *bánh mì*. It's worth it to go out of your way to find *sambal oelek*—one of the best hot sauces on the planet!

1. Combine ¼ cup of the rice wine vinegar in a small bowl with 1 teaspoon of the salt and the sugar. Set aside.

2. Slice the daikon lengthwise into very thin strips—no more than ⅛ inch thick. A mandoline works best, or use a knife and slice really thin. Remember, this will be your wrapper, so you want to keep the strips as thin as possible so that they will be flexible.

3. Lay the strips of daikon on a sheet pan and coat them evenly with the vinegar marinade. Let them sit at room temperature for 20 to 30 minutes.

4. Meanwhile, whisk together the remaining 2 teaspoons rice wine vinegar, the peanut oil, sambal oelek (if using), remaining ½ teaspoon salt, and pepper in a large bowl. Add the tofu, basil, carrots, cilantro, cucumbers, scallions, and jalapeños. Toss to evenly coat the tofu and vegetables in the sauce.

5. Place about four strips of daikon lengthwise on a cutting board so that the long edges overlap each other a bit, forming one large square (think nori for sushi).

(RECIPE CONTINUES)

6. One-quarter of the way up from the bottom edge of the daikon square, place about 2 cups of the tofu strips and vegetables in a horizontal line, then roll up the daikon to enclose the filling like a burrito. It is important to roll as tightly as possible.

7. Repeat step 6 with the remaining strips of daikon and the remaining vegetables. You will likely end up with three or four rolls—the final number will depend on the width of the daikon and the number of strips you slice.

8. Cut each roll in halves or quarters, and serve immediately.

tip: You can find prebaked, Asian-marinated tofu in the vegetarian protein section of your supermarket. Try it chopped and seared in a stir-fry or sliced thin on sandwiches.

french breakfast radishes with nori, tamari, and avocado

PREP TIME: 10 MINUTES,
PLUS 15 MINUTES RESTING TIME
SERVES 2 TO 4

1 pound French Breakfast radishes, greens removed, leaving 1 inch of stem intact

1 teaspoon rice wine vinegar

1½ teaspoons salt

1 avocado, pitted, peeled, and chopped

1 tablespoon freshly squeezed lemon juice

1 tablespoon chopped scallions, white and light green parts only

½ teaspoon freshly ground black pepper

1 sheet nori, cut into thin strips with scissors

2 tablespoons tamari

Our "fancy radish plate," a Vedge signature dish featured in many reviews, is a beautiful display of exotic radishes, roasted, pickled, and marinated, served with smoked tamari and avocado. This recipe captures every bit of the taste in a fraction of the time. French Breakfast radishes are long and thin, with a mild bite. If unavailable, substitute the best-quality radishes you can find. Salting the radishes makes them "sweat," yielding a shiny, lustrous appearance. This makes a gorgeous cocktail party dish or an ideal light summer lunch for two.

1. Cut the radishes in half lengthwise, then toss in a medium bowl with the vinegar and 1 teaspoon of the salt. Set aside at room temperature for at least 15 minutes and up to 30 minutes.

2. Meanwhile, mash the avocado in a medium bowl with the lemon juice, scallions, pepper, and remaining ½ teaspoon salt.

3. Arrange the radishes on a tray. Place 1-inch-round dollops of the avocado salad next to the radishes. Sprinkle the nori strips on top of the radishes and serve the tamari in a ramekin alongside for dipping.

tip: For added crunch and toasty flavor, try garnishing the avocado with toasted black or white sesame seeds.

heirloom tomatoes with grilled shiitakes and green goddess

PREP TIME: 10 MINUTES

COOK TIME: 5 MINUTES

SERVES 2 TO 4

SHIITAKES

10 large shiitake mushrooms, stems removed, caps wiped clean

2 tablespoons olive oil

¼ teaspoon salt

¼ teaspoon freshly ground black pepper

GREEN GODDESS

½ cup loosely packed fresh basil leaves

½ cup vegan mayo

1 tablespoon freshly squeezed lemon juice

1 tablespoon fresh tarragon leaves

2 teaspoons capers, drained

2 teaspoons Dijon mustard

1 medium garlic clove

½ teaspoon salt

½ teaspoon freshly ground black pepper

We chefs start scratching our heads come mid-July when the stockpiles of heirloom tomatoes outpace our ideas of what to do with them. The boring, lazy devil on our shoulders whispers "gazpacho," but that's a temptation I always aim to avoid. I developed this salad as a fun take on the flavors of a classic BLT, and you may find it on the Dirt List at Vedge in late summer. Work to get a nice, crispy char on the shiitakes so that they take on a bacon-like smokiness. Better yet, if you're using an outdoor grill, toss a handful of wood chips on your coals. The throwback green goddess dressing makes use of the abundant summertime basil and could not have a better partner than all those tomatoes.

1. Toss the shiitake caps in a medium bowl with the olive oil, salt, and pepper.

2. Heat a large sauté pan over high heat. Add the shiitake caps and sear them, turning occasionally to prevent burning, until they are crisp, 3 to 5 minutes. If you prefer to use an outdoor grill, first adjust the grates as close together as possible, then grill the shiitake caps until you see clearly defined grill marks, 2 to 3 minutes on each side. In either preparation, remove the mushrooms from the heat, allow them to cool to the touch, then slice into thin strips. Set aside.

3. Combine all of the green goddess ingredients plus 1 tablespoon water in a blender. Blend until smooth.

(INGREDIENTS CONTINUE)

(RECIPE CONTINUES)

4. Slice the tomatoes into thick rounds. Arrange the slices on a serving dish or individual plates, then sprinkle with the olive oil, salt, and pepper.

5. Spoon the dressing on top of the tomatoes. Top with the grilled shiitake slices and a nice handful of the baby salad greens. Serve immediately.

TOMATOES

1 pound heirloom tomatoes or other best-quality tomatoes

1 tablespoon olive oil

¼ teaspoon salt

¼ teaspoon freshly ground black pepper

12 ounces mixed baby salad greens

kohlrabi salad with white beans and horseradish

PREP TIME: 5 MINUTES,
PLUS 30 MINUTES CHILLING TIME
SERVES 4 TO 6

DRESSING

½ cup vegan mayo

½ cup finely sliced red onions

¼ cup Dijon mustard

2 tablespoons capers, drained

2 tablespoons chopped fresh dill

2 tablespoons bottled horseradish

1 tablespoon olive oil

2 teaspoons salt

2 teaspoons freshly ground black pepper

2 teaspoons sherry vinegar

1 teaspoon sugar

3 cups peeled, shredded kohlrabi (about 1 pound)

2 cups cooked cannellini beans *or* one 15-ounce can cannellini beans, rinsed and drained

Kohlrabi, the "German turnip," is a crunchy root vegetable that's delicious raw or cooked. When baked or sautéed, it has a mild broccoli stem–like flavor and luscious creamy texture. Raw, it has a juicy, fresh crunch that we highlight in this punchy, Eastern European–inspired salad. If kohlrabi is unavailable, substitute radishes.

1. Combine all of the dressing ingredients in a large bowl and mix well.

2. Add the kohlrabi and beans to the dressing and toss evenly. Cover and refrigerate the salad for at least 30 minutes (but no longer than 24 hours), then serve.

tip: With the Eastern European influence on this dish and the creaminess of the dressing, an Austrian Grüner Veltliner would be an ideal wine selection. It shows a nice balance of fruit and acid to complement the dill, and its bright aromatics work well with the pungency of the horseradish.

portobello stem
anticuchos

Most people don't know that portobello mushroom stems are often more flavorful than the caps. After roasting portobello mushrooms, you can easily peel open the stems to reveal the stringy, almost meat-like interior. This Latin-inspired *anticucho*, or "food on a stick," is a great party hors d'oeuvre—the recipe doubles or triples easily.

PREP TIME: 10 MINUTES

COOK TIME: 15 MINUTES

SERVES 2 TO 4

1 tablespoon olive oil

2 teaspoons Latin Spice Blend (page 20)

1 teaspoon blackstrap molasses

1 teaspoon tomato paste

1 teaspoon white wine vinegar

8 large portobello mushroom stems

4 wooden skewers, soaked in water

1. Preheat the oven to 400°F.

2. Make the marinade by whisking together the olive oil, Latin Spice Blend, molasses, tomato paste, and vinegar in a medium bowl.

3. Toss the portobello stems in the marinade. Transfer to a sheet pan, reserving any remaining marinade, and roast until soft to the touch, 8 to 10 minutes. Remove the pan from the oven and set aside until the stems are cool enough to handle. Leave the oven on.

4. Make a small slice down the long side of each stem. Pull them open and flatten them out. Skewer the stems widthwise, stretching them out to make them as flat as possible.

5. Brush the skewered stems on both sides with any remaining marinade, return to the pan, and reheat in the oven for 3 to 4 minutes. If you have an outdoor grill, place the skewered mushrooms over high heat for the same amount of time—the flavor and texture will be even better. Serve immediately.

tip: For a simple yet elegant cocktail party, offer these *anticuchos*, *Lupini* Beans with *Piri Piri* (page 41), and one of our Olives recipes (page 27)—they can all be prepared just before your guests arrive. Serve with baguette slices (page 213) and the Sherry Temple (page 222).

In the summer of 2011, after our first restaurant, Horizons, closed but before Vedge opened, Kate and I found ourselves with an uncommon amount of free time. We took an unprecedentedly long vacation, touring Portugal and its Atlantic Islands, stretching from Alentejo down to the Algarve, from Lisbon to Madeira, and finishing up in the Azores. It was on this trip that we discovered what I call the new edamame: *lupini* beans. These peel-and-eat beans, sold in a brine-packed jar, are insanely addictive! At Vedge, we dress them up with fried garlic and *piri piri* sauce. If you can't find Portugal's official hot sauce, try substituting a combination of equal parts sriracha and a New Orleans hot sauce, such as Tabasco or Crystal.

1. Toss the lupini beans in a large bowl with the reserved brine, hot sauce, and pepper. Set aside.

2. Heat the canola oil in a small sauté pan over high heat. When the oil begins to ripple, add the garlic and cook, stirring occasionally to prevent burning, until it turns a dark, golden brown, about 2 minutes.

3. Remove the pan from the heat and pour the browned garlic and its cooking oil over the lupini beans. Stir, then let sit at room temperature for at least 20 minutes and up to an hour before serving.

tip: The outer shell of the *lupini* beans is inedible. Do your guests a favor by demonstrating how to eat them: either pop the bean out of its shell between your teeth or (more politely) twist it out between two pinched fingers and your thumb. Offer a bowl on the side to collect the shells.

lupini beans with *piri piri*

PREP TIME: 5 MINUTES,
PLUS 20 MINUTES RESTING TIME
COOK TIME: 5 MINUTES
SERVES 4 TO 6

One 16-ounce jar lupini beans, drained, 1 tablespoon brine reserved

3 tablespoons piri piri

½ teaspoon freshly ground black pepper

2 tablespoons canola oil

3 large garlic cloves, thinly sliced

roasted rutabaga salad with pistachio and charred onion

PREP TIME: 20 MINUTES

COOK TIME: 20 MINUTES

SERVES 4

1 large rutabaga, peeled

¼ cup plus 2 tablespoons olive oil

1 tablespoon plus 1 teaspoon sherry vinegar

1½ teaspoons salt

1½ teaspoons freshly ground black pepper

1 cup minced onions

2 tablespoons apple cider vinegar

1 teaspoon fresh thyme leaves

2 teaspoons Dijon mustard

4 ounces mixed baby salad greens

¼ cup roasted salted pistachios, crushed

This dish quickly became our signature autumn salad at Vedge. Rutabaga has a lightly sweet and earthy flavor, and a beautiful golden color. In this preparation, we roast it so it gets a little crackly on the edges while remaining tender in the center.

1. Preheat the oven to 450°F.

2. Slice the rutabaga into ⅛-inch-thick slices. A mandoline works best, or use a knife and slice really thin. Lay the slices in a single layer on a sheet pan.

3. Whisk together 1 tablespoon of the olive oil and 1 teaspoon of the sherry vinegar in a small bowl. Use a pastry brush to apply this marinade to the rutabaga slices, then sprinkle them with ½ teaspoon of the salt and ½ teaspoon of the pepper. Roast the rutabaga slices until fork-tender, 7 to 9 minutes. Set aside to cool.

4. Meanwhile, heat 1 tablespoon of the olive oil in a large sauté pan over high heat until it begins to ripple. Carefully add the onions, and sprinkle with ½ teaspoon of the salt and ½ teaspoon of the pepper. Allow the onions to brown and caramelize for 4 to 5 minutes, stirring occasionally. Continue stirring and cooking until the onions have sweated off much of their water and they begin to char, about 3 more minutes. Remove the pan from the heat and deglaze with the apple cider vinegar. Return the pan to the heat and cook until all of the liquid has evaporated but the onions still look very wet. Stir in the thyme leaves, then remove from the heat and set aside to cool.

5. Whisk together the Dijon mustard and the remaining ¼ cup olive oil, 1 tablespoon sherry vinegar, ½ teaspoon salt, and ½ teaspoon pepper in a medium bowl to create the sherry vinaigrette dressing. Add the greens and pistachios and toss to coat.

6. To assemble, arrange three or four rutabaga slices in a circle on each plate. Spoon a tablespoon or two of the charred onions over the rutabagas, and top with a tumble of the dressed greens. Serve.

salt-roasted golden beets with dill, avocado, capers, and red onion

PREP TIME: 10 MINUTES,
PLUS 30 MINUTES CHILLING TIME
COOK TIME: 2 HOURS
SERVES 4 TO 6

This dish takes its cue from lox and bagels. The salt roasting draws out extra moisture and intensifies the flavor of the beets, making them as sweet as candy and as silky as . . . well, something you might have put on a bagel once. Golden beets are quite different from red beets—almost everyone I know loves golden beets even if they don't care for reds. That could be because golden beets are a bit milder. Don't be put off by the cook time, which includes the time to roast the beets. You can take care of the rest of the recipe while the beets are roasting, and it's fine to put other foods along for the ride in the oven—even desserts.

2 cups coarse sea salt or kosher salt

5 pounds golden beets, greens removed

2 tablespoons olive oil

1 tablespoon sherry vinegar

2 teaspoons freshly ground black pepper

1½ cups peeled, seeded, chopped cucumber

¾ cup vegan mayo

½ cup loosely packed fresh dill fronds

1 tablespoon Dijon mustard

½ teaspoon salt

1 avocado, pitted, peeled, and diced

¼ cup capers, drained

¼ cup finely diced red onions

1. Preheat the oven to 300°F.

2. Pour the coarse salt onto a sheet pan, coating the entire bottom of the pan evenly in a thick layer. Arrange the beets in a single layer on the salt. Roast until fork-tender, about 2 hours. The skins will become very dark, looking nearly burnt.

3. Remove the pan from the oven and allow the beets to cool on the salt bed. When cool to the touch, peel the beets by hand or by rubbing them with a towel. Slice them into rounds no more than ⅛ inch thick. A mandoline works best or use a knife to slice them really thin.

4. Toss the beet slices in a large bowl with the oil, sherry vinegar, and 1 teaspoon of the pepper. Cover the bowl and refrigerate for at least 30 minutes but no longer than 24 hours.

5. To prepare the sauce, combine the cucumber, vegan mayo, dill, mustard, salt, and remaining 1 teaspoon pepper in a food processor. Pulse until the cucumber has broken down into very small pieces and the sauce is thick and creamy.

6. Fan the sliced beets on a large platter or on individual plates. Garnish with the avocado, capers, red onions, and a spoonful of the cucumber sauce.

sea bean salad with daikon and cucumber

PREP TIME: 15 MINUTES,
PLUS 30 MINUTES CHILLING TIME
SERVES 4

2 large cucumbers, peeled (about 1½ pounds)

1 large daikon radish, peeled

4 scallions

½ pound sea beans, ends trimmed

3 tablespoons rice wine vinegar

2 tablespoons canola oil

2 tablespoons toasted sesame oil

2 tablespoons tamari

2 teaspoons black sesame seeds

2 teaspoons white sesame seeds

1 teaspoon sugar

2 fresh shiso leaves, finely chopped

When we visited Kyoto, a few hours' ride from Tokyo on the famous Bullet train, we found a little restaurant in the heart of town that won us over with the names of dishes listed on the menu: Firecracker Tofu, Pickled Mixed Radish Salad, and the mysterious sounding *Okonomiyaki*. The chefs were clearly having fun at this place, and we were blown away by the depth of flavor they achieved with such simple preparations. We threw back some sake and tore through plate after plate of food. This salad is inspired by that meal, featuring quirky sea beans (a seaweed-like swamp/beach vegetable) and the haunting flavor of *shiso* (Japanese mint). You can find fresh sea beans at a gourmet market. If they're not available, substitute pencil-thin asparagus. Look for *shiso* in Asian markets, but substitute fresh cilantro if you can't find it.

1. Cut the flesh of the cucumber into very thin noodle-like strips. Avoid the seeds by not cutting the very center of the cucumber. A mandoline works best, or use a knife and slice really thin.

2. Cut the daikon into the same thin noodle-like strips. Here there are no seeds, so you can cut through the entire vegetable.

3. Trim the roots of the scallions, then slice them into fine rings. Start at the white bottom and use about three-quarters of each scallion, until the leaves become much darker green and thicker.

4. Combine the remaining ingredients in a medium bowl to ensure they are well mixed, then add all of the vegetables. Toss to combine, then cover and place in the refrigerator to marinate for at least 30 minutes, but no longer than 24 hours or they will get mushy. Serve chilled.

spiced little carrots with chickpea-sauerkraut puree

I grew up on deli food, and it's usually what I crave from my omnivorous childhood. The one thing I miss the most is a Reuben sandwich, and those flavors are the inspiration for this dish. At the restaurant, we finish young carrots on the grill over wood chips for a nice infusion of smoke. But even when simply baked, as we do here, the flavors in this dish harmonize to create an Eastern European vegetable tribute to the Jewish deli. Serve with a few slices of Warthog Bread (page 214).

1. Preheat the oven to 350°F.

2. In a medium bowl, whisk 2 tablespoons of the olive oil, the steak spice blend, vinegar, ½ teaspoon of the salt, the cloves, and the minced garlic. Add the carrots and toss until combined.

3. Transfer the carrots to a sheet pan, cover with aluminum foil so that they will steam through, and roast until fork-tender, 15 to 18 minutes. Remove the foil and continue to roast until the carrots are soft, an additional 3 to 5 minutes. Remove the pan from the oven and allow the carrots to cool.

4. Meanwhile, to make the puree, combine the chickpeas, sauerkraut and its juice, dill, mustard, pepper, remaining 2 tablespoons olive oil, remaining 1 teaspoon salt, and the smashed garlic clove in a food processor. Process into a smooth, hummus-like consistency.

5. To serve, spread the bean puree onto a serving plate and arrange the carrots, either still warm or fully cooled, on top.

PREP TIME: 15 MINUTES

COOK TIME: 20 MINUTES

SERVES 6 TO 8

4 tablespoons olive oil

1 tablespoon Montreal Steak Spice Blend (page 20)

2 teaspoons sherry vinegar

1½ teaspoons salt

½ teaspoon ground cloves

2 medium garlic cloves, 1 minced and 1 smashed

2 pounds young or baby carrots, tops removed, leaving 1 inch of stem intact (substitute "baby-cut" carrots if necessary)

2 cups cooked chickpeas or one 15-ounce can chickpeas, rinsed and drained

¾ cup bottled sauerkraut with 2 tablespoons of its juice

2 tablespoons minced fresh dill

2 tablespoons Dijon mustard

1 teaspoon freshly ground black pepper

roasted sunchokes with smoked paprika aïoli

PREP TIME: 15 MINUTES

COOK TIME: 10 MINUTES

SERVES 6 TO 8

2 pounds sunchokes

2 tablespoons olive oil

1½ teaspoons salt

1½ teaspoons freshly ground black pepper

1 cup vegan mayo

2 garlic cloves

1 tablespoon Dijon mustard

1 tablespoon smoked paprika

1 teaspoon cumin

¼ cup chopped fresh flat-leaf parsley

Sunchokes—also known as Jerusalem artichokes—are the root of the sunflower plant and one of the few original North American crops. The roots themselves look a bit like ginger but couldn't taste more different. They have a delicate sunflower seed flavor that works well with Middle Eastern, Catalan, and North African flavors. This recipe is a take on *patatas bravas*, a popular tapas dish. Don't peel the sunchokes, as the skins have tons of flavor, and be sure to use smoked paprika for the full Spanish effect.

1. Preheat the oven to 450°F.

2. Cut the sunchokes in halves or quarters depending on their size (each piece should be about 1 inch thick).

3. Toss the sunchokes in a large bowl with the olive oil, 1 teaspoon of the salt, and 1 teaspoon of the pepper.

4. Spread out the sunchokes in a single layer on a sheet pan and roast until fork-tender and the skin begins to crinkle, 8 to 12 minutes.

5. Meanwhile, combine the vegan mayo, garlic, mustard, paprika, cumin, and remaining ½ teaspoon salt and ½ teaspoon pepper in a blender. Blend for a few seconds until the mixture is creamy, drizzling in 2 tablespoons water to emulsify as you blend. Transfer the aïoli to a small ramekin.

6. Remove the sunchokes from the oven, transfer to a large bowl, and toss with the parsley. Serve the warm sunchokes with the aïoli for dipping.

soups and stews

AS A CHILD, it was always the food scenes that lured me into the stories in my books. I mean, who wouldn't want those crazy three-course lunches from *Bread and Jam for Frances*? Cream cheese, tomato and cucumber on rye, cup custard, tomato soup, olives, carrots and celery . . . Frances dined first class!

But the most inspiring story, the one that I carry with me to this day, is *Stone Soup*, the story of a pot of boiling water that slowly builds from stock into a soup by adding vegetables one at a time, creating layers and layers of flavors. There's also some stuff in there about bringing a village together, but what I remember most is the miracle of soup.

I think about that story to this day when I am making the stock that is the basis for so many of our soups at Vedge. Soup is the single uniting dish of the world—every food culture has a "traditional" soup.

What follows is a collection of broths, soups, stews, chowders, and purees. Some come right from the restaurant's repertoire; others are inspired by childhood memories, travel, or trips to farmers markets and specialty stores. Most can be enjoyed all year long, sometimes with a minor substitution; a few work best for a short period of the year, when certain ingredients are at their peak, leaving you to capture that perfect sense of time and place that makes cooking vegetables so satisfying.

pho with roasted butternut squash

PREP TIME: 20 MINUTES

COOK TIME: 45 MINUTES

SERVES 4 TO 6

One 14- to 16-ounce package flat rice noodles

8 cups Vegetable Stock (page 16)

1 cup dried shiitakes

½ cup tamari

2 tablespoons plus 2 teaspoons five-spice powder, preferably Vietnamese (see Tip)

2 teaspoons sugar

½ teaspoon rice wine vinegar

8 to 10 star anise

2 cinnamon sticks

2 garlic cloves

One 1-inch-square piece of ginger, peeled and cut into thirds

4 cups peeled, diced butternut squash (about 2 pounds)

1 cup diced onions

2 tablespoons toasted sesame oil

15 fresh cilantro sprigs

1½ cups bean sprouts

½ cup seeded, thinly sliced jalapeños

Pho is a classic Vietnamese rice noodle soup. It's based on a deeply aromatic, rich broth built with many levels of seasoning. It's nearly impossible to find a vegetarian pho, since bones are used in the classic preparation—in fact, many chefs won't consider a broth made without bones to be true pho. Not me. Vedge's exotic spiced broth is one of my favorite stocks and pairs wonderfully with the tender, sweet roasted squash. Garnishes are traditionally served on the side and added at the table.

1. Place the rice noodles in a large bowl of cold water to soak for 30 minutes. Preheat the oven to 400°F.

2. Meanwhile, combine the Vegetable Stock, shiitakes, tamari, 2 tablespoons of the five-spice powder, the sugar, vinegar, star anise, cinnamon sticks, garlic, and ginger in a large stockpot over high heat. Bring to a boil, reduce the heat, and simmer until the liquid has reduced by one-quarter, 20 to 30 minutes.

3. Toss the squash and onions in a large bowl with the sesame oil and the remaining 2 teaspoons five-spice powder, then spread them out onto a sheet pan. Roast until the squash is fork-tender, about 15 minutes.

4. While the stock is reducing and the squash is roasting, bring a large pot of water to a boil over high heat. Drain the soaking water from the rice noodles and drop them into the boiling water for about 1 minute. Strain again, then divide the noodles evenly among serving bowls.

(RECIPE CONTINUES)

5. Add the roasted squash and onions to the noodles in the serving bowls. Strain the stock through a sieve into the bowls. Stir to combine all of the ingredients, and offer the cilantro sprigs, bean sprouts, and jalapeños alongside as garnishes.

tip: Don't relegate the five-spice powder to the back of your cabinet once you're done making this pho! Five-spice powder also works well with curry powder in tomato-based Indian dishes.

saffron cauliflower soup with *persillade*

PREP TIME: 15 MINUTES

COOK TIME: 35 MINUTES

SERVES 4 TO 6

3 tablespoons olive oil

1 cup finely diced onions

2 tablespoons minced garlic

2 heads cauliflower, leaves and bottoms of stems removed, cut into 1- to 2-inch chunks

1½ teaspoons salt

1 teaspoon freshly ground black pepper

½ cup dry white wine

8 cups Vegetable Stock (page 16)

¼ cup jasmine rice

1 tablespoon Old Bay Seasoning

½ cup diced plum tomatoes

1 teaspoon saffron threads

1 cup fresh flat-leaf parsley leaves

1 tablespoon freshly grated lemon zest

1 garlic clove, smashed

This soup is one of our signature dishes at Vedge. The cauliflower, simmered with tomato, wine, and saffron, then crushed to a rice-like consistency, recalls the flavors of paella. (The secret to getting the right consistency for the cauliflower is to use a potato masher.) Our version of the classic French seasoning mixture *persillade* adds lemon zest, making it closely resemble an Italian gremolata. Either way, its bright, herbal-citrus finish works beautifully with this all-season soup.

1. Heat 2 tablespoons of the oil in a large stockpot over high heat, then add the diced onions and minced garlic. Cook, stirring occasionally to prevent burning, until brown, 3 to 5 minutes.

2. Add the cauliflower chunks, 1 teaspoon of the salt, and the pepper, and continue to brown, stirring occasionally, for another 3 to 5 minutes.

3. Stir in the wine and cook for 2 to 3 minutes.

4. Add the stock, rice, and Old Bay. Bring to a boil, reduce the heat, and simmer, covered, until the cauliflower is fork-tender, 10 to 12 minutes. Stir in the diced tomatoes.

5. Stick your potato masher right into the pot and crush the cauliflower to a rice-like consistency.

6. Stir in the saffron and let steep for 10 to 15 minutes.

7. Meanwhile, make the persillade by chopping the parsley, lemon zest, and garlic to a paste-like consistency. Transfer to a small bowl. Stir in the remaining ½ teaspoon salt and 1 tablespoon olive oil.

8. Ladle the soup into serving bowls and garnish each with a sprinkling of persillade.

(RECIPE CONTINUES)

tip: What could be better than Paris in the springtime? For a bistro menu that could be at home in the garden or at an elegant dinner party in the city, serve this soup along with Shaved Brussels Sprouts with Whole-Grain Mustard Sauce (page 98) and Roasted Baby Turnips with *Maitake* "Champignons au Vin" (page 149). Pair dinner with a Noella Morantin Côt à Côt, a *malbec* from the Loire Valley, and finish the night off with Beetroot *Pots de Crème* (page 179).

peas and carrots with jamaican curry

PREP TIME: 10 MINUTES

COOK TIME: 20 MINUTES

SERVES 4

2 cups shelled fresh English peas (see Tip)

1 pound Thumbelina carrots, peeled

4 tablespoons canola oil

1 teaspoon salt

1 teaspoon freshly ground black pepper

1 tablespoon curry powder

½ teaspoon ground allspice

½ teaspoon ground cumin

¾ cup Vegetable Stock (page 16)

½ cup coconut milk

½ teaspoon light brown sugar

Featuring two vegetables that shared a can throughout my childhood, this curry was inspired by one of our favorite dining experiences at the Sugar Mill restaurant in Montego Bay, Jamaica. Through thoughtful preparation and seasoning, soulful staples like ackee and bean stew and pumpkin soup were elevated to high cuisine. Our curry features a base of island spices and coconut milk that pairs well with rice or pasta and with many vegetables as well. Thumbelina carrots are small and round—about the size and shape of a golf ball—with an especially sweet flavor. If you can't find them, substitute any heirloom carrots, cut into 1½-inch cubes.

1. Preheat the oven to 400°F. Bring a large pot of salted water to a boil over high heat and prepare an ice bath.

2. Blanch the peas in the boiling water for 2 to 3 minutes. Drain the peas, shock in the ice bath for 5 minutes, then drain thoroughly.

3. Toss the carrots in a large bowl with 2 tablespoons of the oil, the salt, and pepper. Spread them on a sheet pan and roast until fork-tender, 12 to 15 minutes.

4. Meanwhile, heat the remaining 2 tablespoons oil in a sauté pan over high heat, then add the curry powder, allspice, and cumin. Allow the spices to sizzle in the oil for about 30 seconds, then stir in the stock, coconut milk, and brown sugar.

5. Simmer for 5 minutes, stir in the peas and roasted carrots, and serve.

tip: Fresh peas really make this dish, but if they are not in season, you can prepare this recipe with thawed frozen peas. Just skip step 2 and add the peas at the beginning of step 5.

Posole is a Mexican stew that uses hominy as its main ingredient. Hominy—dried corn from which the hull and germ have been removed—puffs up to a fluffy, almost dumpling-like texture when cooked. You can cook it in a pressure cooker from its dry state, but it's also available canned, ready to go and easy to work with. This posole also features chayote, a Mexican squash with a mild flavor, and crisp light flesh. The skin is edible, but I recommend removing the pit. (If you can't find chayote, use zucchini instead.) The traditional garnishes for posole are red cabbage and radish, but feel free to experiment with chopped avocado, scallion, jicama, tomato, or whatever else strikes your fancy.

1. Heat the oil in a large stockpot over high heat until it ripples. Add the chayote, poblanos, onions, cumin, garlic, Latin Spice Blend, salt, and pepper and cook, stirring occasionally to prevent burning, until the vegetables are brown, 4 to 6 minutes.

2. Add the stock, hominy, tomatoes, and tomato paste and bring to a boil. Reduce the heat and simmer, stirring often, until the chayote is fork-tender, 10 to 12 minutes.

3. Ladle the posole into serving bowls and garnish with the cilantro, slivered red cabbage, and radishes.

posole with chayote and poblano peppers

PREP TIME: 10 MINUTES
COOK TIME: 15 MINUTES
SERVES 4 TO 6

2 tablespoons canola oil

3 cups pitted, diced chayote (about 2 pounds)

1 cup seeded, chopped poblano peppers

½ cup chopped onions

3 teaspoons ground cumin

2 teaspoons minced garlic

2 teaspoons Latin Spice Blend (page 20)

1½ teaspoons salt

1 teaspoon freshly ground black pepper

6 cups Vegetable Stock (page 16)

3 cups cooked hominy or two 15-ounce cans hominy, drained and rinsed

1 cup diced plum tomatoes

2 teaspoons tomato paste

1 cup packed fresh cilantro leaves

¼ cup slivered red cabbage

¼ cup slivered radishes

puree of chinese broccoli with crushed cucumber and ginger

PREP TIME: 20 MINUTES

COOK TIME: 15 MINUTES

SERVES 4 TO 6

2 teaspoons salt

½ teaspoon freshly ground white pepper

1 pound Chinese broccoli, stems trimmed, leaves roughly chopped

1 cup peeled, chopped cucumbers

½ cup chopped scallions, white and light green parts only

1 teaspoon canola oil

½ teaspoon minced garlic

½ teaspoon minced ginger

½ teaspoon rice wine vinegar

Chinese broccoli is so hearty and flavorful that you can boil the leaves in water with a pinch of salt, puree the mixture, and serve it as soup with nothing else added. In Japan we found many dishes like this one, using the freshest ingredients in simple ways with shockingly complex results. Following the "let your ingredients speak" theory, try to practice restraint here and resist overembellishing an already perfect food.

1. In a large stockpot over high heat, bring 6 cups water to a boil with 1½ teaspoons of the salt and the white pepper. Boil the chopped Chinese broccoli until tender, about 8 minutes. Remove the pot from the heat and set aside to cool. Do not drain.

2. Meanwhile, combine the cucumbers, scallions, oil, garlic, ginger, vinegar, and remaining ½ teaspoon salt in a food processor. Pulse until all of the vegetables are chopped very fine, then transfer to a sieve and let sit for about 10 minutes to drain off the excess liquid.

3. In a few small batches, transfer the Chinese broccoli and cooking liquid to a blender and puree until smooth. Pour each batch as it is blended into another large pot and reheat the soup over medium heat.

4. Ladle the puree into serving bowls and top each serving with a spoonful of the cucumber relish.

hedgehog mushroom, turnip, and barley stew

For the love of pints and pubs . . . drop me anywhere in Ireland or the UK and I will find a home by a fireplace in a cozy chair. Pub food is rich and comforting, but it often needs some imagination to bring it up to modern dining tastes. This take on a classic concept calls for golden hedgehog mushrooms, which come into season just when the weather is starting to get really chilly. Substitute any mushrooms you want, though—even ordinary buttons will shine in this soup.

PREP TIME: 15 MINUTES
COOK TIME: 1 HOUR
SERVES 6 TO 8

1 cup pearl barley, rinsed and drained

3 cups cubed purple or hakurei or standard turnips (about ¾ pound)

1 pound hedgehog mushrooms, stems removed, caps wiped clean

1 cup finely chopped onions

2 tablespoons olive oil

1 tablespoon minced garlic

2 teaspoons salt

1 teaspoon freshly ground black pepper

8 cups Mushroom Stock (page 17)

½ cup dark beer, such as Samuel Smith's Imperial Stout

2 teaspoons chopped fresh thyme

1 teaspoon vegan Worcestershire sauce

2 teaspoons chopped fresh chives

1. Heat 3 cups water in a large saucepan over high heat. When it comes to a boil, add the barley, reduce the heat to medium, and cook until all of the liquid is absorbed, about 40 minutes. Remove the pan from the heat and set aside to cool for at least 20 minutes.

2. Preheat the oven to 450°F.

3. In a large bowl, combine the turnips, mushrooms, onions, olive oil, garlic, salt, and pepper. Toss to distribute the oil, then spread the vegetables on a sheet pan in a single layer and roast until the turnips start to caramelize at the edges, 12 to 15 minutes.

4. Meanwhile, combine the stock, beer, cooked barley, thyme, and vegan Worcestershire sauce in a large stockpot and bring to a boil over high heat. Reduce the heat to a simmer.

5. When the roasted vegetables are done, turn off the heat on the stockpot and carefully transfer the roasted vegetables to the stock.

6. Add the chives, stir the soup, and serve immediately.

fresh chickpea "bourdetto"

PREP TIME: 15 MINUTES

COOK TIME: 15 MINUTES

SERVES 4 TO 6

4 tablespoons olive oil

½ cup finely diced onions

½ cup finely diced red bell peppers

2 tablespoons minced garlic

1 cup finely diced tomatoes

½ cup dry white wine

4 cups fresh chickpeas, shelled (see Tip)

4 cups Vegetable Stock (page 16)

2 teaspoons Old Bay Seasoning

1 teaspoon salt

1 teaspoon freshly ground black pepper

1 teaspoon chopped fresh dill

1 teaspoon chopped fresh oregano or thyme

6 lemon wedges

Bourdetto, a baked fish stew from the island of Corfu, has many variations. At Vedge, we've offered versions with eggplant and oyster mushrooms, but my favorite is this hearty stew that features fresh chickpeas. If you think you like chickpeas, these will take your relationship to the next level. Light green and delicately flavored, fresh chickpeas appear for only a short time each year—if you can't find them, substitute English peas. Try this with a glass of *retsina*—white wine infused with pine resin. It's an acquired taste worth acquiring, and it pairs well with this reinvented nod to Greece.

1. Heat 2 tablespoons of the oil in a medium stockpot over high heat until it ripples. Add the onions, peppers, and garlic and cook, stirring, until brown, 3 to 5 minutes.

2. Add the tomatoes and wine, stir to incorporate, and cook for 4 to 5 minutes to reduce.

3. Add the chickpeas, stock, Old Bay, salt, and pepper. Reduce the heat and simmer until the chickpeas are tender, 8 to 10 minutes.

4. Stir in the dill and oregano and remove the pot from the heat.

5. Serve immediately, garnished with lemon wedges and drizzled with the remaining 2 tablespoons olive oil.

tip: If fresh chickpeas are not in season, you can prepare this recipe with canned chickpeas that have been rinsed and drained. In this case, you will need to simmer for only 5 minutes.

In every great coastal area—be it Brazil, the Mediterranean, San Francisco, or the tropics—there's a signature seafood stew, one that defines the culinary identity of the region: *moqueca*, *bouillabaisse*, *cioppino*, *sopa de mariscos*. At Vedge, we have our own staple meal that we love to serve in the summer, based not on seafood but on an extraordinary type of mushroom, the *honshimeji* or beech mushroom. When I first started working with brown and white beech mushrooms, I was taken by their sea-like flavor. Our reimagined "beach bake" was on the opening menu at Vedge and soon became one of our signature dishes. If corn is out of season, substitute 1 cup cooked or canned white cannellini beans. Serve this alongside our Baguettes (page 213) or other crusty bread.

1. Heat the olive oil in a large stockpot over high heat until it starts to ripple.

2. Add the onions and garlic and cook, stirring, until the onions start to brown, 4 to 6 minutes. Add the mushrooms and brown for an additional 3 to 4 minutes.

3. Pour in the wine and cook until it reduces by half, 3 to 4 minutes.

4. Add the stock, potatoes, tomatoes, Old Bay, salt, and pepper. Shave the corn kernels off the cobs directly into the pot, then bring the mixture to a boil. Reduce the heat and simmer until the potatoes are fork-tender, about 15 minutes.

5. Stir in the chopped thyme, then remove the pot from heat. Serve the stew immediately, garnishing each bowl with fresh thyme sprigs and a final drizzle of olive oil.

honshimeji mushrooms "beach style"

PREP TIME: 15 MINUTES

COOK TIME: 30 MINUTES

SERVES 4 TO 6

2 tablespoons olive oil, plus additional for garnish

1 cup chopped onions

2 tablespoons chopped garlic

2 pounds beech mushrooms, bottoms of stems trimmed, caps wiped clean

½ cup dry white wine

8 cups Vegetable Stock (page 16)

2 cups scrubbed, diced Yukon Gold potatoes

2 cups diced plum tomatoes

3 tablespoons Old Bay Seasoning

1 teaspoon salt

1 teaspoon freshly ground black pepper

3 ears corn

2 teaspoons chopped fresh thyme, plus additional sprigs for garnish

napa cabbage funky kimchi stew

PREP TIME: 10 MINUTES

COOK TIME: 25 MINUTES

SERVES 6 TO 8

2 tablespoons toasted sesame oil

½ cup diced onions

1 tablespoon minced garlic

4 cups finely chopped napa cabbage (about 1 pound)

8 cups Vegetable Stock (page 16)

2 cups vegan kimchi, undrained

¼ cup tamari

2 tablespoons gochujang

2 teaspoons sugar

½ cup finely chopped scallions, white and light green parts only

1 cup peeled, shredded daikon radish (optional)

I wanted to feature a lot of "foodie" dishes on the menu at Vedge so that people would come in for adventurous dining and not just for the vegetable theme. This soup was a risk; it's full of ferment, spice, sour, and funk. Lo and behold, it flies out of the kitchen! Hats off to our guests for trying and embracing this soup. It's worth seeking out the spicy, salty Korean chile bean paste known as *gochujang*, but if you can't find it, substitute a mixture of equal parts chili sauce and miso.

1. Heat the sesame oil in a large stockpot over high heat until it ripples. Add the onions and garlic and cook, stirring, until brown, 3 to 5 minutes.

2. Add the cabbage and continue to brown for an additional 3 to 5 minutes.

3. Add the stock, kimchi with its juice, tamari, gochujang, and sugar and simmer for 15 minutes, stirring often.

4. Serve in bowls, garnished with scallions and daikon, if desired.

tip: *Gochujang* is an essential condiment in Korean restaurants—we like to use it as a spicy spread on Asian-style wraps and sandwiches.

lentil mulligatawny with cilantro-onion salad

PREP TIME: 15 MINUTES,
PLUS 30 MINUTES CHILLING TIME
COOK TIME: 30 MINUTES
SERVES 6 TO 8

1½ cups packed fresh cilantro leaves

½ cup finely chopped red onions

½ cup finely sliced scallions, white and light green parts only

2 tablespoons plus ½ teaspoon canola oil

2 tablespoons freshly squeezed lemon juice

½ teaspoon salt

1 cup minced onions

1 tablespoon minced garlic

2 tablespoons curry powder

8 cups Vegetable Stock (page 16)

1 cup dried golden lentils, picked through and rinsed

Indian food is comfort food for Kate and me. When we are travel weary, all we can think about is getting home for some good Indian takeout, and this soup is one of our favorites. Mulligatawny, or "pepper water," is a soup that the British adapted from a Southeast Indian lentil and rice dish. Our recipe calls for golden lentils, though you could substitute red if you like. The bright salad garnish is packed with onion and lemon, building levels of flavor to complement the cooked cilantro. This works as a main-course soup when accompanied by rice and greens.

1. Combine 1 cup of the cilantro, the red onions, scallions, ½ teaspoon of the canola oil, the lemon juice, and the salt in a small bowl. Cover and refrigerate for at least 30 minutes but no longer than 24 hours.

2. Heat the remaining 2 tablespoons canola oil in a large stockpot over high heat until it ripples. Add the minced onions and garlic and cook, stirring, until brown, 3 to 5 minutes.

3. Add the curry powder and let it sizzle in the oil for about 2 minutes, stirring occasionally to prevent burning.

4. Add the stock and lentils. Bring to a boil, reduce the heat, and simmer for approximately 20 minutes, stirring often, until the lentils are tender.

5. Transfer 6 cups of the soup to a blender. Add the remaining ½ cup cilantro and blend.

6. Return the blended mixture to the stockpot and stir well to combine.

7. Serve the soup in bowls, garnished with the chilled cilantro-onion salad.

Long before the Jersey Shore became a reality show, the seaside in summertime was a way of life for Philadelphians. Most of us have fond memories of our childhood visits to Brigantine, Cape May, Margate, Seaside Heights, and Avalon. The ocean air inspires me. It's when I'm running barefoot at the water's edge that I come up with my best menu ideas. Many, like this one, are born out of my love for summer and all things coastal. The French touches of sherry and tarragon play against the light sea-flavor of the oyster mushrooms while the texture of the corn with the potatoes will instantly recall every great chowder you have enjoyed at the beach.

1. Heat the olive oil in a large stockpot over high heat until it ripples. Add the mushrooms, onions, garlic, salt, and pepper and cook, stirring occasionally to prevent burning, until brown, 3 to 5 minutes.

2. Add the sherry and cook until it reduces by one-quarter, about 2 minutes.

3. Add the stock, potatoes, celery, and Old Bay. Shave the corn kernels off the cobs directly into the pot, then bring to a boil. Reduce the heat and simmer until the potatoes are fork-tender, 8 to 12 minutes.

4. Stir in the vegan sour cream, thyme, and tarragon and simmer for an additional 2 to 3 minutes. Serve immediately.

oyster mushroom and corn chowder

PREP TIME: 15 MINUTES

COOK TIME: 20 MINUTES

SERVES 6 TO 8

2 tablespoons olive oil

1 pound oyster mushrooms, bottoms of stems trimmed, caps wiped clean

½ cup diced onions

2 teaspoons minced garlic

1 teaspoon salt

1 teaspoon freshly ground black pepper

½ cup sherry

8 cups Vegetable Stock (page 16)

1 cup scrubbed, diced Yukon Gold potatoes

½ cup diced celery

2 tablespoons Old Bay Seasoning

4 ears corn

½ cup vegan sour cream

2 teaspoons chopped fresh thyme

1 teaspoon chopped fresh tarragon

parsnip and chestnut bisque with mulled wine–spiced onion confit

PREP TIME: 15 MINUTES

COOK TIME: 1 HOUR

SERVES 4 TO 6

This soup, spiked with seasonal and festive flavor combinations, was inspired by a holiday visit to the Terrace Restaurant in Longwood Gardens, a botanical garden about a half hour south of Philadelphia. Part of its magic is the mulled wine, infused with traditional Christmas spices: cinnamon, cloves, nutmeg. The nuttiness of the chestnuts combined with the aromatic parsnips yields a rich, creamy puree as the perfect canvas for the spices. Make your life easy and buy pre-peeled chestnuts in a package or can.

BISQUE

2 tablespoons olive oil

2 cups slivered onions

2 pounds parsnips, peeled and roughly chopped

12 cups Vegetable Stock (page 16)

2 cups peeled, chopped chestnuts

2 teaspoons salt

1 teaspoon freshly ground black pepper

¼ cup vegan sour cream

1. To start the base for the soup, heat the olive oil in a large stockpot over high heat until it starts to ripple. Add the slivered onions and cook, stirring, until brown, 4 to 6 minutes.

2. Add the parsnips and continue cooking, stirring, for another 5 to 7 minutes.

3. Add the stock, chestnuts, salt, and pepper. Bring to a boil, reduce the heat, and simmer until the parsnips are fork-tender, 12 to 15 minutes.

4. Stir in the vegan sour cream and remove the pot from the heat.

5. Transfer the soup in batches to a blender and puree, emptying each batch into another large pot. Once all of the soup has been blended, put the pot over very low heat to keep warm.

(RECIPE CONTINUES)

(INGREDIENTS CONTINUE)

CONFIT

1 tablespoon olive oil

½ cup chopped onions

½ teaspoon salt

½ teaspoon freshly ground black pepper

½ teaspoon sugar

¼ teaspoon ground cinnamon

¼ teaspoon ground cloves

¼ teaspoon ground nutmeg

1 cup red wine, preferably Cabernet Sauvignon

6. Heat the olive oil in a sauté pan over high heat until it ripples. Add the chopped onions and cook, stirring, until brown, about 4 minutes.

7. Reduce the heat to medium-low, then stir in the salt, pepper, sugar, cinnamon, cloves, and nutmeg. Let the spices cook with the chopped onions for 2 to 3 minutes, stirring occasionally to prevent burning.

8. Add the red wine and reduce completely, leaving no liquid in the pan with the onions, 5 to 7 minutes. Then continue to cook the onions until they are very soft and sweet, about 15 minutes more.

9. To serve, ladle the hot soup into bowls and garnish with the onion confit.

soba bowl with shiitake *dashi* and market greens

PREP TIME: 10 MINUTES

COOK TIME: 10 MINUTES

SERVES 4

Of all the Japanese-inspired recipes in this book, this one is the mother: the most basic expression of culinary simplicity. Though soba noodles contain varying amounts of wheat flour, their base is buckwheat, which lends an extra dimension of flavor. As for the greens, we like spinach, kale, or bok choy, but you can use whatever you have on hand—even lettuces or cabbage will work. This dish is our breakfast most mornings!

1 pound greens, stems removed, large leaves chopped

4 bundles dried soba or udon noodles

8 cups Shiitake Dashi (page 17)

4 teaspoons toasted sesame oil

2 tablespoons chopped scallions, white and light green parts only

2 teaspoons sesame seeds

½ sheet nori, cut into ⅛-inch-wide strips with scissors

1. Bring a large stockpot of water to a boil over high heat. Blanch the greens for about 2 minutes. Use a sieve or tongs to transfer the greens to a plate. Leave the water boiling.

2. Cook the noodles in the same boiling water according to the package instructions, typically 4 to 6 minutes for al dente.

3. In a large pot, bring the Shiitake Dashi up to a simmer.

4. Meanwhile, divide the sesame oil among four serving bowls, then portion the greens into the bowls on top of the sesame oil.

5. Drain the noodles into a colander and portion them directly on top of the greens.

6. Ladle the Shiitake Dashi over the noodles. Garnish with scallions, sesame seeds, and nori. Serve immediately.

spring bean stew

PREP TIME: 15 MINUTES

COOK TIME: 20 MINUTES

SERVES 4

2 tablespoons olive oil

2 cups slivered spring onions, such as scallions or baby leeks

1 tablespoon minced garlic

1 pound fresh spring beans, such as fava or lima, shelled

1 teaspoon salt

1 teaspoon freshly ground black pepper

8 cups Vegetable Stock (page 16)

½ cup quartered cherry tomatoes

1 teaspoon chopped fresh tarragon

1 teaspoon chopped fresh thyme

Early in the spring and throughout the summer, we come across all kinds of fresh beans. When favas, limas, chick-peas, and even English peas are cooked just until they're bright green and still have a little crunch left in them, they truly taste like a garden. Spring onions, such as scallions or baby leeks, add a touch of heat and sweetness to balance out this ode to spring. If you're using fava beans, keep in mind that they have another shell on the bean itself that must be peeled away. It takes some extra time but is well worth it.

1. Heat the olive oil in a large stockpot over medium heat. Add the spring onions and garlic and cook, stirring, until brown, about 3 minutes.

2. Add the spring beans, salt, and pepper. Stir and brown for an additional 5 minutes.

3. Add the stock and cherry tomatoes and simmer until the beans are slightly tender, about 8 minutes.

4. Remove from the heat, stir in the chopped fresh herbs, and serve.

shanghai bok choy and okinawa hot pot with spicy miso broth

PREP TIME: 15 MINUTES

COOK TIME: 20 MINUTES

SERVES 4 TO 6

This recipe calls for two of my favorite Asian vegetables: Shanghai bok choy (or bok choy shoots) and Okinawa sweet potatoes. Okinawas have a striking purple and white marbled flesh and a nutty, lightly sweet flavor. If you live near an Asian market, by all means seek these out. If not, you can substitute any mild sweet potato. The spicy miso broth is easy to execute and will likely become a standard in your soup repertoire.

4 cups scrubbed, diced Okinawa sweet potatoes (about 2 pounds)

2 tablespoons toasted sesame oil

1 teaspoon salt

1 teaspoon freshly ground black pepper

8 cups Shiitake Dashi (page 17)

2 tablespoons white miso paste

1 tablespoon minced garlic

1 tablespoon sriracha

1 pound Shanghai bok choy, left whole, or standard bok choy, cut into ½-inch pieces

½ cup chopped scallions, white and light green parts only

1. Preheat the oven to 400°F.

2. In a large bowl, toss the sweet potatoes with the sesame oil, salt, and pepper. Transfer them to a sheet pan and roast until fork-tender, 10 to 12 minutes.

3. Combine the Shiitake Dashi, miso paste, garlic, and sriracha in a large stockpot over high heat. Bring to a boil, reduce the heat, and simmer for 5 minutes. Reduce the heat to low until the potatoes finish roasting.

4. Stir the bok choy, scallions, and roasted sweet potatoes into the soup and cook for 2 minutes.

5. Ladle the soup into bowls and serve.

peruvian squash and giant lima bean stew

PREP TIME: 20 MINUTES

COOK TIME: 20 MINUTES

SERVES 6 TO 8

2 tablespoons olive oil

½ cup chopped red onions

1 tablespoon minced garlic

3 tablespoons creamy peanut butter

2 teaspoons ground cumin

2 teaspoons salt

2 teaspoons freshly ground black pepper

8 cups Vegetable Stock (page 16)

2 teaspoons tamari

1 teaspoon sugar

4 cups peeled, diced winter squash, such as kabocha, butternut, or acorn (about 2 to 3 pounds)

3 cups fresh lima beans

1 cup chopped plum tomatoes

½ cup packed, chopped fresh cilantro

½ teaspoon crushed red pepper flakes

⅓ cup black olives, pitted and chopped (optional)

1 lime, cut into wedges

Peru, the country that gave the world the potato (thank you!), also gave us the flavor combination of olive, cilantro, peanut, and lime. Shaking your head? I did too when I tried to imagine how they would taste together. The salty sweetness of the olives combined with peanut, zesty cilantro, and tangy lime is extraordinary. Fresh lima beans really make this dish, but if they are not available you can prepare this recipe with thawed frozen beans.

1. Heat the oil in a large stockpot over high heat until it ripples. Add the onions and garlic and cook, stirring, until brown, 3 to 5 minutes.

2. Stir in the peanut butter, cumin, salt, and pepper and cook for an additional 2 minutes, stirring occasionally to prevent burning. Add the Vegetable Stock, tamari, and sugar, then stir to incorporate the peanut butter evenly.

3. Add the squash, bring to a boil, and reduce the heat to low. Simmer until fork-tender, 10 to 12 minutes.

4. Add the lima beans, tomatoes, ¼ cup of the cilantro, and the red pepper flakes. Stir and bring back to a simmer for 5 minutes.

5. Portion the soup into bowls and garnish with the remaining ¼ cup cilantro, olives (if desired), and lime wedges.

the dirt list

IN 2008, I was introduced to a guy who is, indirectly, responsible for the creation of Vedge. His name is Casey Spacht, and he runs Lancaster Farm Fresh, a co-op of small farms in central Pennsylvania.

The day Casey brought me a sample box of vegetables from his co-op, it was clear that it had been picked that morning. Carrots with their bright green leaves still attached, fennel with beads of water on it that looked juicy enough to bite into like an apple. Swiss chard so crisp you could snap a leaf off! This was produce!

And the flavor! These were vegetables that tasted like vegetables—sweet and juicy, with an undercurrent of earthiness you can get only when your food has just been pulled from the garden. From the moment I tasted that offering of vegetables from Casey,

anything else tasted like the cardboard box it was packed in.

Immediately, my culinary focus began to change from the style of cuisine (vegan) to the actual food itself (vegetables). The Dirt List was born from this concept: fresh seasonal vegetables—much of it less than twenty-four hours out of the ground—cooked simply, yet embellished with clever garnishes to add a special twist. By keeping each vegetable true to its self, the results have been extraordinary.

Since Vedge has opened, we have served more than 2,000 new dishes on our Dirt List. The following recipes—mostly lifted from these daily Dirt Lists—make standout side dishes, or you can combine three or four for a memorable meal.

broccoli rabe philly style

PREP TIME: 15 MINUTES

COOK TIME: 20 MINUTES

SERVES 2 TO 4

3 tablespoons olive oil, plus more for oiling pan

4 red bell peppers

2 teaspoons balsamic vinegar

1¼ teaspoons salt

1¼ teaspoons freshly ground black pepper

2 bunches broccoli rabe, bottom 3 inches of stems removed, leaves and remaining stems chopped into 1-inch pieces

2 tablespoons minced garlic

1 tablespoon porcini powder

½ cup vegan mayo

1 teaspoon Dijon mustard

Sliced bread, toasted or grilled (optional)

With its green awnings, mural art, and scent of red gravy in the air, Philly's famous Italian Market is practically un-changed since it appeared in the original *Rocky* movie back in the seventies. Stroll down 9th Street, and you're bound to find my favorite traditional Italian greens, broccoli rabe. Not the easiest vegetable to work with, it can quickly become a bitter mess if not prepared properly. The key is blanching first and draining all excess water, then knowing when to stop cooking—when it's just one shade darker than it was just after blanching. In addition, broccoli rabe must be really fresh. If it's started to wilt, move on to another green.

In this recipe, I'm recommending some other classic South Philly flavors: dried porcini and roasted peppers. If you live near Philadelphia, try to get an authentic Amoroso hoagie roll (what the cheesesteaks are served on). Alterna-tively, this dish can be served as an elegant antipasto with olives.

1. Preheat the oven to 400°F. Bring a large pot of salted water to a boil over heat high and prepare an ice bath.

2. Rub a sheet pan lightly with olive oil. Put the peppers on the pan and roast until they collapse, 12 to 15 minutes. Remove the peppers from the oven and set aside until cool to the touch. Peel off the skins, cut the peppers in half, and remove the seeds and stems. Then slice the peppers into thin strips and toss in a small bowl with 1 table-spoon of the oil, the balsamic vinegar, ½ teaspoon of the salt, and ½ teaspoon of the pepper. Set aside.

3. Blanch the broccoli rabe in the salted boiling water for 4 minutes. Reserve 2 tablespoons of the cooking water. Drain the broccoli rabe, shock in the ice bath for 5 minutes, then drain thoroughly.

(RECIPE CONTINUES)

4. Heat the remaining 2 tablespoons oil in a large sauté pan over high heat. When it begins to ripple, add the garlic and allow it to brown for about 1 minute. Add the broccoli rabe, ½ teaspoon of the salt, and ½ teaspoon of the pepper. Cook, stirring often, until the broccoli rabe wilts and turns a slightly darker shade of green, 5 to 7 minutes, then remove the pan from the heat.

5. Meanwhile, whisk the porcini powder with the reserved 2 tablespoons cooking water in a small bowl. Add the vegan mayo, mustard, and remaining ¼ teaspoon salt and ¼ teaspoon pepper and whisk until creamy.

6. If desired, spread the cream on the bread and top with the broccoli rabe and peppers. Or, if serving the broccoli rabe and peppers as an antipasto, offer the cream on the side.

Like many people, for years I considered Greek cuisine a cliché of salads and spanakopita, hummus and gyros. Our discovery of true Greek cuisine over the years has been deliciously eye opening. Truly the most underappreciated of all Mediterranean cuisines, it is one of the healthiest on the planet and full of unique flavors floating on luscious layers of olive oil and lemon. *Horta*, very simply, are braised greens with garlic in olive oil and lemon. We've paired them here with *skordalia*, an addictive dip made from bread, potatoes, and a nice hit of garlic. If dandelion greens are unavailable, substitute arugula.

1. Preheat the oven to 400°F.

2. Puncture the potato with a fork three times, sprinkle with the coarse sea salt, and wrap individually in foil. Bake until tender to the touch, about 40 minutes.

3. Remove the potato from the oven, unwrap it, and let it cool. When cool enough to handle, cut it into 1-inch chunks.

4. Make the skordalia by combining the potato chunks, bread cubes, garlic clove, olive oil, sherry vinegar, salt, pepper, and ¾ cup water in a food processor. Pulse until smooth. Set aside.

5. To make the horta, heat the canola oil in a large pot over high heat. Before it starts to ripple, add the chopped garlic and brown for 2 to 3 minutes. Add 1 cup water, then the greens, salt, and pepper. Cook until the greens wilt, 6 to 8 minutes, then stir in the lemon juice and olive oil. Remove the pot from the heat.

6. Serve the greens with a scoop of the skordalia.

dandelion greens *horta* with *skordalia*

PREP TIME: 15 MINUTES

COOK TIME: 50 MINUTES

SERVES 4

SKORDALIA

1 russet potato, scrubbed

½ teaspoon coarse sea salt

2 cups stale bread cubes

1 garlic clove

½ cup olive oil

2 teaspoons sherry vinegar

1 teaspoon salt

1 teaspoon freshly ground black pepper

HORTA

2 teaspoons canola oil

2 tablespoons chopped garlic

2 pounds dandelion greens, chopped

2 teaspoons salt

2 teaspoons freshly ground black pepper

¼ cup freshly squeezed lemon juice

2 tablespoons olive oil

fingerling potatoes with creamy worcestershire sauce

PREP TIME: 10 MINUTES

COOK TIME: 15 MINUTES

SERVES 2 TO 4

1 pound fingerling potatoes, scrubbed

2 tablespoons olive oil

1½ teaspoons salt

1½ teaspoons freshly ground black pepper

½ cup vegan mayo

2 tablespoons vegan Worcestershire sauce

1 tablespoon Dijon mustard

2 teaspoons sherry vinegar or malt vinegar

1 teaspoon sugar

Fingerling potatoes are small in size but they pack all the flavor of larger potatoes. With their greater skin-to-flesh ratio, we focus on the tasty potato skin here and cloak it in a rich and tangy sauce that wraps the punch of Worcestershire in a creamy blanket of vegan mayo. It's Classic Pub Fare 101.

1. Preheat the oven to 400°F.

2. Toss the potatoes in a large bowl with the olive oil, 1 teaspoon of the salt, and 1 teaspoon of the pepper. Transfer to a sheet pan and roast until fork-tender, 12 to 15 minutes. Remove the pan from the oven and allow the potatoes to cool on the pan for just a bit.

3. Meanwhile, in a food processor, combine the vegan mayo, vegan Worcestershire sauce, mustard, vinegar, sugar, and remaining ½ teaspoon salt and ½ teaspoon pepper. Pulse until smooth.

4. Toss the warm potatoes in a medium bowl with the sauce. Serve immediately.

tip: For other alternatives to mashed potatoes, try Savoy Cabbage Colcannon (page 95) and Whipped Salsify with Red Wine and Truffle *Jus* (page 109).

red potato "ash" with sauce *gribiche*

PREP TIME: 15 MINUTES

COOK TIME: 45 MINUTES

SERVES 2 TO 4

GRIBICHE

½ cup vegan mayo

½ cup chopped pickles or cornichons

2 tablespoons capers, drained

2 tablespoons Dijon mustard

2 tablespoons chopped fresh flat-leaf parsley

1 tablespoon olive oil

1 tablespoon chopped fresh tarragon

2 teaspoons salt

2 teaspoons freshly ground black pepper

POTATOES

2 pounds red potatoes, scrubbed

2 tablespoons canola oil

1 tablespoon chopped fresh thyme

1 teaspoon salt

1 teaspoon freshly ground black pepper

For all you charcoal grillers out there, the "ash" in the title of this recipe refers to cooking in foil directly on hot coals. When the potatoes come out, they are smoky, meaty, and incredibly tender. *Gribiche*, a close relative of rémoulade, is a classic French sauce of chunky vegetables bound in mayo. Think of this dish as a new take on potato salad. It also makes a great veggie dip for crudité.

1. Combine all of the gribiche ingredients in a food processor. Add 1 tablespoon water and pulse to a coarse consistency. Transfer to an airtight container and chill in the refrigerator for up to 5 days.

2. Bring a large pot of salted water to a boil over high heat. Add the potatoes and boil until they are just fork-tender but not fully cooked through, 12 to 15 minutes.

3. Drain the potatoes thoroughly and toss in the pot with the oil, thyme, salt, and pepper.

4. Lift off the grates of your charcoal grill, then set it to high. Alternatively, preheat your oven to 350°F.

5. Create a double-layer pouch of aluminum foil, fill it with the potatoes, and fold it shut.

6. Place the package directly on the coals of the grill and leave it there for 3 minutes while the heat of the grill warms it through. Turn off the heat, then leave the package resting on the coals for 25 minutes. If you are using an oven, roast at 350°F for 35 to 40 minutes.

7. Remove the foil, carefully remove the potatoes, and serve them warm with the gribiche on the side.

grilled baby bok choy with tamari and chinese mustard sauce

PREP TIME: 10 MINUTES

COOK TIME: 15 MINUTES

SERVES 4 TO 6

1 pound baby bok choy, halved lengthwise

2 tablespoons toasted sesame oil

1 teaspoon salt

¼ cup vegan mayo

2 tablespoons Chinese mustard (see Tip)

2 tablespoons canola oil

2 teaspoons tamari

1 teaspoon rice wine vinegar

Bok choy has always been my definitive stir-fry vegetable. The juicy, white stems yield a satisfying crunch, and the leafy green tops offer a slightly sweet, nutty flavor. But because of these opposite textures, grilling the entire vegetable at once requires skill and attention. Careful placement on the grill allows you to cook the stems through, while only lightly cooking the leaves. The effect is spectacular, showcasing two very different results from a single vegetable. Buy the smallest bok choy you can find for this recipe; the flavor is better concentrated, and they are easier to grill properly.

1. Preheat the grill to the highest setting or preheat a grill pan over high heat.

2. Toss the bok choy halves in a large bowl with the sesame oil and salt until evenly coated. Place the dressed bok choy on the grill or grill pan with the thicker bases on hotter spots (near the center) and the leaves on cooler spots (near the edges) to achieve even grilling. Allow the bok choy to char for about 3 minutes on each side.

3. To make the sauce, whisk together the vegan mayo, mustard, canola oil, tamari, vinegar, and 2 tablespoons water in a medium bowl.

4. Serve the bok choy right off the grill with a dollop of the mustard sauce.

tip: Please don't use leftover Chinese restaurant delivery packets of hot mustard here! Instead, pick up a small jar of the real stuff next time you're in the Asian aisle of the supermarket. The extra kick of spice you get from Chinese mustard adds body and flavor to an Asian salad dressing, or combine it with some vegan mayo for a wonderfully pungent condiment for sandwiches and crudité.

hakurei turnips with falafel crumbs and creamy sesame

PREP TIME: 20 MINUTES,
PLUS 20 MINUTES RESTING TIME
COOK TIME: 25 MINUTES
SERVES 4

FALAFEL CRUMBS

1 cup chickpea flour

2 teaspoons olive oil

1 teaspoon ground cumin

½ teaspoon curry powder

½ teaspoon salt

½ teaspoon freshly ground black pepper

¼ teaspoon ground coriander

TURNIPS

1 pound hakurei turnips, greens removed, leaving 1 inch of stem intact

2 tablespoons olive oil

1 teaspoon minced garlic

1 teaspoon salt

1 teaspoon freshly ground black pepper

Poor turnips, too often relegated to the "soup stock" bag in supermarkets, with a carrot, an onion, and a sprig of wilted parsley as their only friends. Granted, they can be challenging to prepare properly, and they become bitter if they are not extremely fresh. So, if you are trying to convince yourself of their merits or to win over a turnip-hater, try to find *hakureis*—these beauties with a sweet, mild flavor are also known as Tokyo turnips. (If *hakureis* are unavailable, simply cut standard turnips into 1½-inch chunks.) In this recipe, they prove their versatility when dressed up with some Middle Eastern flourishes. Can you tell that the inspiration for this dish comes from a falafel sandwich?

1. Preheat the oven to 400°F.

2. To make the falafel crumbs, whisk together the chickpea flour, oil, cumin, curry powder, salt, pepper, coriander, and ⅓ cup water in a medium bowl. Let stand for 20 minutes.

3. Spread the mixture in a thin layer on a sheet pan and bake until it turns golden brown, 8 to 10 minutes. Set aside until cool enough to handle. Separate the mixture into rough chunks and return to the oven to bake for an additional 5 minutes.

4. Let cool again, then crumble into ¼-inch crumbs. If you're not proceeding with the rest of the recipe immediately, store the crumbs in an airtight container at room temperature for up to 3 days.

5. Preheat the oven to 400°F if it's not still on from making the crumbs.

(INGREDIENTS CONTINUE)

(RECIPE CONTINUES)

6. Cut any larger turnips in half through the stem to achieve uniform size for even roasting. Toss the turnips in a medium bowl with the oil, garlic, salt, and pepper.

7. Transfer the turnips to a sheet pan and roast until fork-tender and the edges start to crinkle, 8 to 10 minutes.

8. Meanwhile, make the creamy sesame by whisking together the vegan mayo, tahini, vinegar, salt, pepper, and 3 tablespoons water in a medium bowl until smooth and creamy.

9. Use a large spoon to smear the creamy sesame neatly on a serving plate.

10. Arrange the roasted turnips on top of the creamy sesame, sprinkle with the falafel crumbs, and serve.

CREAMY SESAME

¼ cup vegan mayo

¼ cup tahini

1 teaspoon rice wine vinegar

¼ teaspoon salt

¼ teaspoon freshly ground black pepper

Nebrodinis are soft, fleshy Italian mushrooms with a very delicate flavor. In this dish, however, we focus on their amazing texture. Sliced thin, they mimic the texture of *fazzoletti* pasta, affectionately known as "little handkerchiefs." Lightly sautéing them, as you would with actual pasta, provides a unique canvas that takes perfectly to this basil sauce. A light tomato sauce would work well, too. If *nebrodinis* are unavailable, substitute king oyster mushrooms or royal trumpets.

PREP TIME: 20 MINUTES

COOK TIME: 10 MINUTES

SERVES 4 TO 6

1 cup packed fresh basil leaves

1 cup Vegetable Stock (page 16)

2 garlic cloves

4 tablespoons olive oil

1 tablespoon dry white wine

1 teaspoon salt

1 teaspoon freshly ground black pepper

1 pound nebrodini mushrooms, wiped clean

2 cups halved grape or cherry tomatoes

1. To make the basil sauce, combine the basil, vegetable stock, garlic, 2 tablespoons of the olive oil, the wine, ½ teaspoon of the salt, and ½ teaspoon of the pepper in a food processor. Puree until smooth and set aside.

2. Slice the nebrodini mushrooms as thinly as possible using a mandoline or knife.

3. Heat the remaining 2 tablespoons olive oil in a large skillet or two large sauté pans over high heat. (More surface area will allow for more even cooking on such thin slices.) When the oil starts to ripple, add the mushroom slices. Sprinkle with the remaining ½ teaspoon salt and ½ teaspoon pepper. Allow the mushrooms to cook for 6 to 8 minutes, stirring as necessary for even browning.

4. Add the basil sauce and tomatoes to the pan and continue cooking for 2 to 3 minutes. Remove from the heat and serve.

roasted asparagus with hazelnut *picada*

PREP TIME: 15 MINUTES

COOK TIME: 15 MINUTES

SERVES 4 TO 6

Picada is one of Spain's great sauces. It can be creamy like tahini or coarse and crumbly, like our version here. We use hazelnuts, but substitute almonds if you prefer. For the asparagus spears, I recommend the French technique of peeling the bottom one-third in order to utilize the whole vegetable. (If you prefer to cut off the bottoms, be sure to save them for vegetable stock.) Keep in mind that asparagus does a significant amount of carryover cooking once removed from the heat, so always pull it out while it's still bright green to account for that extra "cooking."

¼ cup stale bread cubes

¼ cup shelled, skinned unsalted hazelnuts

3 tablespoons olive oil

2 teaspoons minced garlic

1 teaspoon salt

1 teaspoon freshly ground black pepper

1 teaspoon chopped fresh thyme

2 bunches asparagus, bottom one-third trimmed with a peeler to achieve uniform thickness (about 2 pounds)

1. Preheat the oven to 400°F.

2. Toss the bread cubes and hazelnuts in a small bowl with 1 tablespoon of the olive oil, the garlic, ½ teaspoon of the salt, and ½ teaspoon of the pepper. Transfer the mixture to a sheet pan and roast until browned, about 8 minutes. Remove from the oven and toss with the thyme. Cool slightly before transferring to a food processor. Pulse into a crumble.

3. Meanwhile, toss the asparagus in a large bowl with the remaining 2 tablespoons olive oil, ½ teaspoon salt, and ½ teaspoon pepper. Transfer to a sheet pan and roast until bright green and lightly crinkled, about 4 minutes for pencil-thin asparagus or up to 10 minutes for jumbo spears.

4. Serve the asparagus immediately with the picada sprinkled on top.

roasted cauliflower with black vinegar and kimchi cream

PREP TIME: 10 MINUTES

COOK TIME: 10 MINUTES

SERVES 2 TO 4

1 head cauliflower

2 tablespoons canola oil

1 teaspoon salt

1 teaspoon freshly ground black pepper

2 tablespoons Chinese black vinegar

½ cup vegan mayo

¼ cup vegan kimchi, undrained

Sometimes the most pedestrian of vegetables can be the most interesting. Cauliflower makes a fantastic canvas for bold sauces. Here we take it for a spicy ride with Chinese black vinegar and Korean kimchi, yet the flavor of the cauliflower shines through. The black vinegar's acidity is balanced by the sweetness of dried fruit, and its flavor is unmistakable. This recipe uses just enough kimchi to add an addictive, salty burst of funky flavor—give it a try if you've been wary up till now.

1. Preheat the oven to 450°F.

2. Chop the cauliflower head in half, remove the leaves, and cut a V shape into the bottom of each half to remove the core. Slice the remaining sections into florets with about 1 inch of stem.

3. Toss the cauliflower florets in a medium bowl with the canola oil, ½ teaspoon of the salt, and the pepper. Transfer to a sheet pan and bake until the edges start to char and caramelize, 8 to 10 minutes.

4. Remove the cauliflower and return it to the bowl. Toss evenly with the black vinegar, if using.

5. Meanwhile, to make the kimchi cream, combine the vegan mayo, the kimchi with its juice, and the remaining ½ teaspoon salt in a food processor. Pulse until the kimchi breaks down into small chunks and is evenly distributed throughout the mayo.

6. Serve the cauliflower hot from the oven over a pool of the kimchi cream.

Anyone who has been to Vedge knows that we love radishes. In this elegant dish, we celebrate watermelon radishes. Slice these beauties open and you will be treated to a colorful pinwheel of red, white, and green. Some of that color will fade in the light cooking that we suggest in this recipe but the radishes will take on an amazing texture that pairs well with the spring flavors of fava beans and tarragon. Carpaccio traditionally refers to extremely thin slices of cured meat. These days, it's a term that refers to a very thin cut of almost anything—the process makes an easy transition into the vegetable world in this dish. Conceived in the spring of 2012, this is one of my favorite Dirt List items.

watermelon radish carpaccio with fava beans and tarragon

PREP TIME: 20 MINUTES

COOK TIME: 20 MINUTES

SERVES 4 TO 6

1 pound watermelon radishes, peeled

3 tablespoons olive oil

1 teaspoon salt

1 teaspoon freshly ground black pepper

2 tablespoons finely sliced shallots

2 teaspoons minced garlic

¼ cup dry white wine

1½ cups Vegetable Stock (page 16)

2 cups shelled fava beans

¼ cup finely sliced scallions, white and light green parts only

2 tablespoons chopped fresh tarragon

1 teaspoon nigella seeds

1. Preheat the oven to 300°F.

2. Slice the radishes as thinly as possible. A mandoline works best, or use a knife and slice really thin. Toss the radishes in a medium bowl with 1 tablespoon of the olive oil, ½ teaspoon of the salt, and ½ teaspoon of the pepper.

3. Transfer the radish slices to a sheet pan and bake until slightly tender, 6 to 8 minutes.

4. Meanwhile, heat 1 tablespoon of the olive oil in a large sauté pan over high heat. Add the shallots, garlic, and remaining ½ teaspoon salt and ½ teaspoon pepper and cook, stirring, until brown, 3 to 5 minutes.

5. Add the wine and reduce by half, 3 to 5 minutes.

6. Add the Vegetable Stock and bring to a simmer. Add the fava beans and cook for 4 to 5 minutes.

7. Stir in the scallions, tarragon, nigella seeds, and remaining 1 tablespoon olive oil. Remove the pan from the heat.

8. Using shallow bowls or plates that have a defined edge to capture the light broth, arrange the radishes in single layers, covering the entire bottoms of the dishes. Spoon a portion of the broth in the center of each serving, allowing the beans to pile up and the sauce to run toward the outer edges of the radishes.

roasted *kabocha* squash with black trumpet mushrooms and madeira

PREP TIME: 25 MINUTES

COOK TIME: 25 MINUTES

SERVES 4 TO 6

4 cups peeled, diced kabocha squash (2 to 3 pounds)

3 tablespoons olive oil

1 teaspoon salt

1 teaspoon freshly ground black pepper

½ pound black trumpet mushrooms, wiped clean

½ cup chopped shallots

2 teaspoons minced garlic

½ cup Madeira

½ cup Vegetable Stock (page 16)

1 teaspoon chopped fresh rosemary

This is a "first taste of autumn" dish for me. It's late October, the tomatoes are gone, the eggplants and peppers are dwindling down, and there's a distinct nip in the air. This time of year I start craving those deeper, heartier flavors that one just doesn't get at summer picnics and barbecues. Black trumpet mushrooms are a delicious harbinger of chilly weather and holidays. They have a deep, nutty, and intensely earthy flavor that complements the rich, soft flesh of cold-weather squash like the *kabocha* here. (Feel free to substitute chanterelles or brown beech mushrooms for the black trumpets, and acorn or butternut squash for the *kabocha*.) The sweet, raisin-like flavor of Madeira takes the whole dish home.

1. Preheat the oven to 400°F.

2. Toss the squash in a large bowl with 2 tablespoons of the olive oil, ½ teaspoon of the salt, and ½ teaspoon of the pepper. Transfer to a sheet pan and roast until fork-tender, 8 to 12 minutes.

3. Meanwhile, heat the remaining 1 tablespoon olive oil in a large sauté pan over high heat. Add the mushrooms, shallots, garlic, and remaining ½ teaspoon salt and ½ teaspoon pepper and cook, stirring occasionally, until evenly brown, 5 to 7 minutes.

4. Deglaze the mushrooms with the Madeira and reduce by half, 3 to 5 minutes.

5. Add the Vegetable Stock and rosemary, stir, then remove from the heat.

6. Arrange the squash in a serving dish. Spoon the mushrooms over the squash and serve.

savoy cabbage colcannon

PREP TIME: 20 MINUTES

COOK TIME: 15 MINUTES

SERVES 6 TO 8

1 medium head savoy cabbage, heart removed and discarded, leaves cut into 1-inch chunks

1 medium onion, finely diced

1 teaspoon minced garlic

4 tablespoons olive oil

1½ teaspoons salt

1½ teaspoons freshly ground black pepper

4 cups peeled Yukon Gold potatoes, cut into 1-inch round slices (2 to 3 pounds)

¾ ounce fresh chives

¼ cup vegan sour cream

The famous Irish dish colcannon is traditionally made with cabbage or kale and mashed potatoes. I was dying to reinvent this classic, so I envisioned a healthy at-home version, tinted bright green by the addition of a last-minute chive emulsion. Of course, the temptation here is to also add more fat. But who needs it? Savoy cabbage is already a flavorful vegetable, and by roasting it, we coax out even more flavor. The result is delicious—but light enough for you to have an extra pint.

1. Preheat the oven to 400°F.

2. Toss the cabbage, onion, and garlic with 2 tablespoons of the oil, 1 teaspoon of the salt, and 1 teaspoon of the pepper. Transfer to a sheet pan and roast until the cabbage edges turn brown, 5 to 8 minutes. Set aside.

3. Bring a medium pot of salted water to a boil over high heat. Cook the potatoes until fork-tender, 8 to 10 minutes. Drain the potatoes, reserving ½ cup of the cooking water. Set aside.

4. Meanwhile, combine the chives with the remaining 2 tablespoons oil, ½ teaspoon salt, ½ teaspoon pepper, and ⅓ cup water (not the reserved cooking water) in a blender. Blend until smooth. Set aside.

5. Combine the roasted cabbage and potatoes in a large bowl. Add the chive oil, reserved cooking water, and vegan sour cream. Stir, letting the potatoes mash a bit while making sure the chive oil evenly coats the potatoes and cabbage. Serve immediately.

seared french beans with caper *bagna cauda*

PREP TIME: 10 MINUTES

COOK TIME: 5 MINUTES

SERVES 4 TO 6

In preparing *bagna cauda*, a warm Italian oil dip with a paste of garlic and capers (and anchovies), you mash or puree the vegetables with more olive oil than they can hold until the oil separates and becomes boldly infused with the flavors of the vegetables. Our favorite experience with *bagna cauda* was in an unlikely place—Japan—where we were served a miso *bagna cauda* that inspired us to create this version. Try replacing the thin French green beans with asparagus or broccolini.

½ cup plus 2 tablespoons olive oil

3 garlic cloves

2 tablespoons capers, drained

3 teaspoons freshly ground black pepper

2 teaspoons salt

1 teaspoon chopped fresh thyme

1 pound green beans, preferably haricots verts, ends trimmed

4 lemon wedges (optional)

1. Combine ½ cup of the olive oil, the garlic, capers, 2 teaspoons of the pepper, 1 teaspoon of the salt, and the thyme in a food processor. Pulse until the mixture has a paste-like consistency. Set aside.

2. Heat the remaining 2 tablespoons olive oil in a large skillet over high heat. When the oil begins to ripple, add the green beans, sprinkle with the remaining 1 teaspoon salt and 1 teaspoon pepper, and sear the beans until the skins get crinkly, 4 to 5 minutes. Turn the beans as little as possible to achieve a nice, even sear.

3. Transfer the beans to a serving dish and spoon the bagna cauda on top. Garnish with the lemon wedges if desired.

shaved brussels sprouts with whole-grain mustard sauce

PREP TIME: 15 MINUTES

COOK TIME: 10 MINUTES

SERVES 2 TO 3

½ cup vegan mayo

2 tablespoons whole-grain mustard

1 teaspoon salt

1 teaspoon freshly ground black pepper

1 pound Brussels sprouts, 2 or 3 layers of outer leaves removed and bottom cores cut off

2 tablespoons olive oil

2 teaspoons minced garlic

Brussels sprouts were one of my personal challenges when we opened Vedge; I was never very fond of them. But as we prepared to open a vegetable restaurant, I vowed to prepare any vegetable, even ones I didn't like very much, in ways everyone could enjoy. This recipe is a result of that effort, and I can honestly say that I now love Brussels sprouts. It has everything to do with shaving them. That texture, mingling with the creamy, tangy mustard sauce, recalls a warm Caesar salad. On our menu since we opened, this dish is one of our most popular.

1. To make the sauce, whisk together the vegan mayo, mustard, 1 tablespoon water, ½ teaspoon of the salt, and ½ teaspoon of the pepper in a small bowl. Set aside.

2. Run the Brussels sprouts through the slicer blade of a food processor or carefully shave on a mandoline.

3. Heat the olive oil in a large sauté pan over high heat. Just as the oil starts to ripple, add the garlic and the shaved Brussels sprouts. Sear for 30 seconds, then stir to prevent the garlic from burning.

4. Add the remaining ½ teaspoon salt and ½ teaspoon pepper, then allow the Brussels sprouts to sear for 4 to 5 minutes, stirring occasionally so they brown evenly.

5. Transfer the Brussels sprouts to a serving dish, drizzle the mustard sauce on top, and serve.

I get greedy and impatient with corn. Who can wait for Jersey corn? The Florida corn starts in late winter, the Georgia corn in April, and my favorite, Carolina corn, comes in May. If you have access to an outdoor grill, please try the "On the Cob" method for a nice outdoor barbecue. Looking for an extra kick? Substitute jalapeños for the poblanos. Or, for an irresistible summer soup, served hot or cold, puree it all with 4 cups of Vegetable Stock (page 16).

summer corn with green chile cream

PREP TIME: 10 MINUTES

COOK TIME: 15 MINUTES

SERVES 4 TO 6

4 ears corn

½ cup finely chopped seeded poblano peppers

¼ cup finely chopped onions

1 tablespoon canola oil

1 teaspoon salt

1 teaspoon freshly ground black pepper

2 tablespoons vegan sour cream

1 tablespoon chopped fresh cilantro

OVEN METHOD

1. Preheat the oven to 400°F.

2. Shave the corn kernels off the cobs into a large bowl and toss with the poblanos, onions, canola oil, salt, and pepper. Transfer the mixture to a sheet pan and bake until the top of the mixture starts to char, about 15 minutes.

3. Return the mixture to the bowl. Fold in the vegan sour cream, cilantro, and 2 tablespoons water, then serve.

"ON THE COB" METHOD

1. Preheat the grill to high.

2. Brush the shucked ears of corn with 1½ teaspoons of the canola oil, then grill the ears directly on the grill racks until lightly charred on all sides, 4 to 8 minutes.

3. Meanwhile, heat the remaining 1½ teaspoons canola oil in a large sauté pan over high. When it starts to ripple, add the poblanos, onions, salt, and pepper. Cook, stirring, until brown, 3 to 5 minutes. Stir in the vegan sour cream and 2 tablespoons water and cook for an additional 2 to 3 minutes. Remove from the heat and stir in the cilantro.

4. Serve the ears of grilled corn drizzled with the green chile cream.

swiss chard with pickled golden raisins and pistachios

PREP TIME: 10 MINUTES

COOK TIME: 20 MINUTES

SERVES 2 TO 4

½ cup rice wine vinegar

¼ cup golden raisins

1½ teaspoons sugar

1 teaspoon salt

2 bunches Swiss chard, large center stalks removed, leaves chopped (about 1 pound)

2 tablespoons canola oil

2 teaspoons chopped garlic

½ teaspoon freshly ground black pepper

2 tablespoons roughly chopped pistachios

Greens with nuts and fruit is a common Italian flavor combination. We first came to appreciate this tradition in Sardinia when dining al fresco at a charming little restaurant perched on top of a hill in the Old Town section of Alghero, sipping a simple Canaiolo (what locals call Grenache). Our most captivating food memory that evening was the plate of grilled vegetables, drizzled with a sweet-sour-salty punch of aged balsamic and pistachios. This dish captures the elements I loved most in that dish. By pickling the golden raisins, we temper their sweetness while adding a new dimension of bright acid to the greens.

1. Combine the vinegar, raisins, sugar, and ½ teaspoon of the salt in a medium saucepan over high heat. Bring to a boil, reduce the heat, and simmer for 5 minutes. Set aside to cool.

2. Meanwhile, bring a large pot of salted water to a boil over high heat and prepare an ice bath. Add the chard to the boiling water and blanch for 3 minutes. Drain the chard, shock in the ice bath for 5 minutes, then drain thoroughly.

3. Heat the canola oil in a large sauté pan over high heat. As it begins to ripple, add the garlic and cook until brown, 2 to 3 minutes. Add the chard, pepper, and remaining ½ teaspoon salt. Cook until the chard wilts, 5 to 7 minutes.

4. Transfer the chard to a serving dish. Drain the raisins from their pickling liquid. Garnish the chard with the raisins and pistachios, then serve.

(RECIPE CONTINUES)

tip: Spanning Tuscany to Sicily, here is a menu that will please everyone. Tell your guests you are serving Italian, and enjoy as they're blown away by the unique flavors in this dish, along with *Nebrodini* Mushrooms as *Fazzoletti* (page 87), and Eggplant Braciole (page 159), served with Gavi, an Italian white wine from Piedmont. Our current favorite comes from Cascina degli Ulivi. Enjoy a glass before bringing out the Caramel *Panna Cotta* with Red Raspberries and Tarragon (page 183) which also comes from the Piedmont region of Italy.

tatsoi with "seawater" broth

PREP TIME: 5 MINUTES

COOK TIME: 15 MINUTES

SERVES 2 TO 4

1 pound tatsoi, bottoms trimmed

1 ounce kombu seaweed

½ ounce dry wakame seaweed, broken into pieces (see Tip)

½ teaspoon salt

¼ teaspoon tamari

A member of the mustard green family, *tatsoi* has a delicious flavor and crunchy texture that remind me of a cross between curly spinach and bok choy. Look for *tatsoi* in Asian markets, but substitute bok choy or green chard if you can't find it. The simple sea-scented broth is an expression of restraint and simplicity, inspired by dishes we ate in Tokyo and Kyoto. This is definitely a dish for a Zen-like mood rather than a Super Bowl party. Try it with steamed rice and pickled vegetables on a sick day when you want to warm and nourish your body—perhaps the day after the Super Bowl party!

1. Bring 3 cups lightly salted water to a boil in a medium stockpot over high heat and prepare an ice bath. Blanch the tatsoi for 2 to 3 minutes. Use tongs or a sieve to transfer the tatsoi to the ice bath. Shock in the ice bath for 5 minutes, then drain thoroughly. Leave the water boiling.

2. To make the seawater broth, add the kombu, wakame pieces, salt, and tamari to the tatsoi cooking water. Reduce the heat and simmer for 10 minutes. Remove the kombu.

3. Reheat the tatsoi in the hot broth. Portion the tatsoi into serving bowls, pour the seawater broth on top, and serve.

tip: Dry wakame seaweed may require a trip to your local health food store, but it's worth it. It will last forever in your pantry, and it lends excellent flavor and saltiness to Asian broths, not to mention B vitamins.

seared yellow wax beans with *togarashi*

PREP TIME: 15 MINUTES

COOK TIME: 10 MINUTES

SERVES 4

1 tablespoon crushed red pepper flakes

1 tablespoon black sesame seeds

1 tablespoon white sesame seeds

¼ sheet nori

1½ teaspoons salt

1½ teaspoons freshly ground black pepper

2 tablespoons canola oil

1 pound yellow wax beans, ends trimmed

In Japan, many restaurants set the table with a curious little wooden condiment box that includes a mysterious red powder. My friends, meet the new "in" spice blend: *togarashi*. At its most basic, it's crushed red chile peppers. But as it becomes more complex, one will find orange peel, seaweed, sesame, and ginger mixed in. It's a great way to add heat with flavor. Here we pair it with crisp yellow wax beans for a mind-blowing midsummer bar snack, but you'll get equally tasty results from green beans.

1. To make the togarashi, combine the red pepper flakes, black and white sesame seeds, and nori in a spice mill and pulse until coarse. (A clean coffee bean grinder or a mortar and pestle would work well, too.) Transfer the mixture to a small bowl, stir in the salt and pepper, and set aside.

2. Heat the oil in a large skillet or two large sauté pans over high heat. (More surface area will allow for more even cooking.)

3. Just before the oil heats to the smoking point, carefully add the beans. It is important for the beans to get a nice sear, so you might prefer to do this step in two batches depending on the size of your pan(s). Allow the beans to sear for 2 minutes until you see some blistering, then turn with tongs, and continue to sear for another 2 minutes.

4. Add 2 tablespoons of the togarashi to the beans. Remove the pan from the heat and toss the beans to distribute the spice blend evenly. Serve immediately.

Ramp season. The spring appearance of these "wild leeks" marks one of the most anticipated culinary moments of the year. You finally get some, look at them, and wonder what the big deal is all about—it's just a big leaf on a skinny scallion! Then you cook them, and the doors to onion heaven open and shine their light. By the time you figure out what to do with all your ramps, ramp season is done. However, we came up with this warm ramp hummus in the 2012 season, and we stopped right there. This is one of my favorite dishes in Vedge's history, a fun and unique way to introduce ramps to someone who has never had them before. (And you can always substitute leeks if it isn't ramp season.) Serve with bread, pita, chips, or raw veggies.

1. To make the hummus, combine the chickpeas, garlic, lemon juice, ¼ cup of the olive oil, ¾ cup water, 1 teaspoon of the salt, 1 teaspoon of the pepper, and the cumin in a food processor. Pulse until the mixture is smooth and creamy.

2. Heat the remaining 2 tablespoons oil in a large sauté pan over high heat until it ripples. Add the ramps and the remaining ½ teaspoon salt and ½ teaspoon pepper. Cook until the leaves have thoroughly wilted, 3 to 5 minutes, then remove from the heat. Stir in the sherry vinegar and ¼ cup water.

3. Transfer the hummus to a serving dish and make a small well in the center. Pour the ramp mixture into the well along with all its cooking juices. Serve immediately with your choice of dipping items.

warm ramp hummus

PREP TIME: 15 MINUTES

COOK TIME: 5 MINUTES

SERVES 4 TO 6

3 cups cooked or canned chickpeas, drained and rinsed

2 garlic cloves

¼ cup freshly squeezed lemon juice

¼ cup plus 2 tablespoons olive oil

1½ teaspoons salt

1½ teaspoons freshly ground black pepper

½ teaspoon ground cumin

2 cups ramps, white parts finely chopped and leaves cut into 1-inch lengths

1 tablespoon sherry vinegar

whipped salsify with red wine and truffle *jus*

PREP TIME: 20 MINUTES

COOK TIME: 45 MINUTES

SERVES 8

2 pounds salsify, peeled and cut into 1-inch-thick chunks

½ cup vegan mayo

3 tablespoons olive oil

1 teaspoon freshly ground black pepper

1 cup finely chopped onions

½ cup dry red wine

1 teaspoon salt

¾ cup Vegetable Stock (page 16)

1 tablespoon white truffle oil

1 teaspoon chopped fresh thyme

Salsify's that weird-looking root vegetable at the market that you never see anyone pick up and put in their basket. It's one of those poor, misunderstood European vegetables that just hasn't caught on here—yet. But peel it down and roast it, fry it, or puree it, and you will be surprised by its creamy texture and unique, nutty flavor. Think of this dish as a funky take on mashed potatoes and gravy. Parsnips make a nice substitution if you can't find salsify, taking the dish in a slightly sweeter direction.

1. Bring a large pot of salted water to a boil over high heat. Cook the salsify until fork-tender, about 15 minutes. Use a slotted spoon to transfer the salsify to a large bowl, and measure out 4 cups of the cooking water.

2. In a few small batches, transfer the salsify and 4 cups cooking water to a blender and blend until smooth and creamy. As each batch is done, empty the contents of the blender into a large bowl. When all of the salsify is blended, whisk in the vegan mayo, 1 tablespoon of the olive oil, and ½ teaspoon of the pepper. Divide the puree among eight individual ramekins or transfer it all to one 13 x 9-inch casserole dish.

3. Heat the remaining 2 tablespoons olive oil in a medium saucepan over high heat. When it begins to ripple, add the onions and cook, stirring, until brown, 3 to 5 minutes. Add the wine, salt, and remaining ½ teaspoon pepper and reduce by half, 3 to 5 minutes. Add the Vegetable Stock, reduce the heat, and simmer for 5 minutes. Remove the pan from the heat and stir in the truffle oil and thyme.

4. Preheat the broiler. Broil the salsify until the top begins to brown, 8 to 12 minutes.

5. Drizzle the red wine sauce on top of the salsify and serve.

greens

YOU CAN TELL a lot about a chef by how well they cook their greens. Do they obliterate their baby spinach and does their kale take twenty minutes to chew? Or do they masterfully wilt their baby greens and strike the perfect balance between leaf and stem in the heartier ones?

Greens are nutritious, and when prepared well, they are delicious. Sauteéd greens with garlic and olive oil are one of the simplest and most exquisite pleasures in life. Eating greens should be an indulgence, not a chore. Here are a few tips to keep it that way:

■ Greens are unforgiving: you cannot fix them once they're past their prime. With that in mind, always buy the absolute freshest product possible.

■ Learn to cook them just right; taste them often as you go. Undercooking can leave a grassy, leafy taste in your mouth, while overcooking can produce a bitter, gray mess.

■ Blanch heavier greens like broccoli rabe, kale, and Swiss chard. Boil them for 3 minutes, drain them, transfer them to an ice bath, drain, and *then* sauté. You'll be shocked at what a difference this makes.

baby scarlet turnips and their greens with garlic *jus*

PREP TIME: 5 MINUTES
COOK TIME: 15 MINUTES
SERVES 2 TO 4

1 pound baby scarlet turnips with their greens

2 tablespoons olive oil

2 teaspoons salt

2 teaspoons freshly ground black pepper

2 tablespoons minced garlic

The turnip, a relative of the radish, is not the easiest vegetable to love. Its beautiful white flesh leads one to believe that it will have the creamy richness of celery root or parsnips. While it does make a surprisingly light and almost fluffy puree, its flavor can sometimes be a bit astringent, which is why turnips must be used only when they are very fresh. Enter the baby scarlet turnip, with its bright, sweet flavor and crisp greens—it will make you a turnip lover after one bite. This dish is built around the natural flavors of baby scarlet turnips, but if you can't find them, just use standard turnips, cut into 2-inch chunks.

1. Preheat the oven to 400°F. Bring a large pot of salted water to a boil over high heat and prepare an ice bath.

2. Chop the greens off the turnips, leaving about 1 inch of the stems intact. Chop the greens into 1-inch lengths. Set aside the greens.

3. In a medium bowl, toss the turnips with 1 tablespoon of the oil, 1 teaspoon of the salt, and 1 teaspoon of the pepper. Transfer to a sheet pan and roast until fork-tender, 6 to 8 minutes. Remove from the oven and set aside to cool.

4. Meanwhile, blanch the chopped greens in the boiling water for 2 minutes. Drain the greens, shock in the ice bath for 5 minutes, then drain thoroughly.

5. In a large sauté pan, heat the remaining 1 tablespoon oil just until it ripples. Add the garlic and cook, stirring, until it is light brown, 3 to 5 minutes. Remove from the heat, then deglaze the pan with ½ cup water. Add the blanched greens to the pan, return to the heat, and heat through, 2 to 3 minutes, making sure not to overcook them.

(RECIPE CONTINUES)

6. Transfer the greens and jus to a serving dish and arrange the roasted turnips on top. Serve immediately.

tip: Once you use the whole vegetable, you'll never go back—remember, most clean scraps can be used for Vegetable Stock (page 16), and if this recipe has turned you into a turnip lover, check out a dish that has become a favorite on our Dirt List: *Hakurei* Turnips with Falafel Crumbs and Creamy Sesame (page 84).

marinated *chioggia* beets and their greens with nigella seeds and sherry vinegar

PREP TIME: 5 MINUTES,
PLUS 15 MINUTES RESTING TIME
COOK TIME: 15 TO 30 MINUTES
SERVES 2 TO 4

1 large bunch Chioggia beets, their greens separated (1 to 2 pounds)

¼ cup canola oil

¼ cup sherry vinegar

2 teaspoons nigella seeds

1 teaspoon salt

1 teaspoon freshly ground black pepper

Journalists love to ask chefs what their favorite new ingredient is—it's an interesting question because the answers are always changing. My latest obsession is nigella seed. Known also as black cumin or wild onion seed, it offers an exotic flavor and a crunchy texture to your cooking. Try experimenting with it in recipes from any spice-forward cuisine like Indian, Moroccan, or Middle Eastern. Here, they pack a little punch of earthy pungency on top of the sweet candy-striped *Chioggia* beets. If *Chioggia* beets are unavailable, standard beets will work just fine in this recipe.

1. Bring a large pot of salted water to a boil over high heat and prepare an ice bath. Blanch the greens for 2 minutes. Use tongs or a sieve to transfer the greens to the ice bath. Shock in the ice bath for 5 minutes, then drain thoroughly. Leave the water boiling.

2. Using the same boiling water, boil the beets until fork-tender, anywhere from 12 to 30 minutes depending on the size of the beets. Drain the beets and set them aside to cool.

3. Meanwhile, combine the oil, vinegar, nigella seeds, salt, and pepper in a medium bowl. Toss the blanched greens in this dressing.

4. Rub the warm beets with a kitchen towel to remove the skin without dyeing your fingers. Dice them into 1-inch cubes and toss in the vinaigrette with the greens. Let stand at least 15 minutes or up to 2 hours, then serve.

grilled broccolini with pistachio, cured olive, and preserved lemon

PREP TIME: 15 MINUTES

COOK TIME: 15 MINUTES

SERVES 2 TO 4

¼ cup olive oil

1 teaspoon chopped preserved lemon

1 tablespoon juice from preserved lemon

1 teaspoon sugar

1 teaspoon salt

1 teaspoon freshly ground black pepper

1 cup pistachios

1 pound broccolini, 2 inches of the bottom stems removed

2 tablespoons canola oil

½ cup chopped oil-cured olives

1 cup wood chips for charcoal grill use (optional)

Broccolini is a cross between traditional and Chinese broccoli. It has a long edible stem and delicious broccoli-like florets on top. While this makes it a bit tricky to cook (cooking the stems through without overcooking the florets), it's relatively easy to make this delicious green shine. This preparation is the best I've found so far: blanching and then grilling. You can even grill it ahead of time, refrigerate it, and serve it cool or at room temperature. If you use wood chips in a charcoal grill, the flavor is astonishingly deep and smoky. We treat it with some Moroccan flourishes here, but purists will love it with just a little olive oil and lemon. This method works just as well with broccoli rabe if you can't find broccolini.

1. Bring a large pot of salted water to a boil over high heat and prepare an ice bath.

2. To prepare the vinaigrette, combine the olive oil, chopped preserved lemon and juice, sugar, ½ teaspoon of the salt, and ½ teaspoon of the pepper in a food processor. Puree until smooth. Set aside.

3. In a large sauté pan over medium heat, dry-toast the pistachios until they begin to brown slightly and become very fragrant, 3 to 5 minutes. Remove from the heat. When the pistachios are cool to the touch, chop them roughly. Set aside.

4. Drop the broccolini into the boiling water and blanch for 4 minutes. Drain the broccolini, shock it in the ice bath for 5 minutes, then drain thoroughly.

5. Heat a grill pan or outdoor charcoal grill to high. If you're using a charcoal grill, soak the wood chips in water for 3 minutes while the grill is heating. Then, drain the wood chips and carefully place them directly on the coals, under the grates.

(RECIPE CONTINUES)

6. Toss the blanched broccolini in a large bowl with the canola oil and the remaining ½ teaspoon salt and ½ teaspoon pepper. Grill the broccolini in a single layer until it chars slightly, 4 to 7 minutes, turning after 2 to 3 minutes.

7. Arrange the broccolini on a serving tray. Drizzle with the preserved lemon vinaigrette and sprinkle with the chopped pistachios and chopped olives.

white eggplant with catalan spices and saffron aïoli

PREP TIME: 15 MINUTES

COOK TIME: 20 MINUTES

SERVES 4 TO 6

4 white eggplants, halved lengthwise

5 tablespoons olive oil

2 tablespoons sherry vinegar

1½ teaspoons salt

1½ teaspoons freshly ground black pepper

1 teaspoon ground cumin

½ teaspoon smoked paprika

Pinch of ground cloves

½ teaspoon saffron threads soaked in ¼ cup warm water for about 5 minutes

1 cup vegan mayo

2 garlic cloves

Calling all eggplant skeptics: you have to try white eggplant. The soft, sweet flesh is so melt-in-your-mouth tender that it will erase all of your nightmares of bitter, seedy, chewy purple eggplant. Here is a Catalan-style recipe from our tapas-hopping trip to Barcelona and Mallorca. You can substitute Japanese eggplant in this recipe, but make sure to buy the freshest eggplant possible. Any sign of wrinkles on the skin? Just move on.

1. Preheat the oven to 400°F.

2. Place the eggplants, fleshy sides up, on a sheet pan. Use a paring knife to lightly score the tops with two or three Xs.

3. Whisk together 4 tablespoons of the oil, the vinegar, 1 teaspoon of the salt, 1 teaspoon of the pepper, the cumin, paprika, and cloves in a small bowl. Using a pastry brush, apply the mixture to the scored flesh of the eggplant halves.

4. Roast the eggplant halves until the edges start to brown, 8 to 12 minutes. Turn the eggplant halves over and roast until they are cooked all the way through and tender, another 2 to 3 minutes.

5. Meanwhile, to make the aïoli, combine the saffron and its soaking water with the vegan mayo, garlic, remaining 1 tablespoon olive oil, and remaining ½ teaspoon salt and ½ teaspoon pepper in a blender. Blend until smooth and creamy.

6. Serve the eggplant warm out of the oven with a dollop of the aïoli.

tip: Any leftover aïoli can be refrigerated in an airtight container for up to 1 week. It's delicious anywhere you'd use mayonnaise—as a spread on sandwiches, with crudité, or for dipping French fries.

"Pesto *Trapanese*" were the words I heard over and over again during the summer before Vedge opened. My chef de cuisine was on a mission to feature this underappreciated and underused Sicilian sauce on a Vedge menu. We finally found a home for it on zucchini and never looked back. Zucchini has the perfect texture to carry the thick sauce, and the roasted tomato and nuts with the basil add depth.

1. Preheat the oven to 400°F.

2. Heat 2 tablespoons of the olive oil in a large sauté pan over high heat. Just as it starts to ripple, add the tomatoes and almonds and allow the tomatoes to brown and blister for 4 to 5 minutes, stirring occasionally. Remove the pan from the heat and let cool completely.

3. To make the pesto *Trapanese*, transfer the cooled tomatoes and almonds to a food processor and add the basil, garlic, salt, pepper, ½ cup water, and the remaining 2 tablespoons olive oil. Pulse until all of the basil leaves are broken down and the sauce is thick and creamy.

4. Arrange the zucchini in a 13 x 9-inch casserole dish in three or four layers. Pour the pesto *Trapanese* on top of the zucchini slices, making sure that all of the slices are completely covered. Bake until the sauce bubbles, 8 to 10 minutes. Serve immediately.

zucchini with pesto *trapanese*

PREP TIME: 15 MINUTES

COOK TIME: 15 MINUTES

SERVES 4 TO 6

4 tablespoons olive oil

1 cup cherry tomatoes

½ cup raw almonds

1 cup packed fresh basil leaves

1 tablespoon chopped garlic

1 teaspoon salt

1 teaspoon freshly ground black pepper

2 zucchini, sliced into thin rounds (about 1 pound)

plates (aka mains)

AT VEDGE, WE offer a variety of "plates" that allow our guests to choose what type of dining experience they want to have on a particular evening. Our plates are the size of a traditional appetizer, perhaps a little bigger. Some guests share a plate or two for a quick, casual bite at the bar. Others, sitting down to dinner, order four or more plates per person. Not only does this permit a lively and social dining experi-ence, but it broadens the range of our menu that each guest gets to sample.

Not every home cook has the time or energy to do the prep that goes into all of the labor-intensive plates we make at the restaurant. For certain dishes, we have blown them up to make full-size main courses, perfect for home cooks to serve from their kitchens without spending the entire day prepping.

hearts of palm cakes on curried lentils

PREP TIME: 20 MINUTES

COOK TIME: 35 MINUTES

SERVES 4

Hearts of palm are unsung heros in the vegetable world. Vedge's hearts of palm hail from the Wailea Agricultural Group on the big island of Hawaii. Sustainably farmed and flown to us each week, fresh hearts of palm have a flavor and texture that can't be beat. Their crunchy, clean-tasting white flesh is reminiscent of a fresh artichoke heart. If you don't have a small tropical farm filling your produce orders on a weekly basis, canned or jarred hearts of palm make for a very good runner-up.

2 tablespoons olive oil

2 tablespoons minced green bell peppers

2 tablespoons minced scallions, white and light green parts only

One 16-ounce can hearts of palm, drained, cut into 2-inch chunks

4 teaspoons curry powder

1 teaspoon salt

¼ cup minced onions

4 cups Vegetable Stock (page 16)

1 cup dried yellow or red lentils, picked through and rinsed

2 tablespoons chopped fresh cilantro

½ cup vegan mayo

1. Heat 1 tablespoon of the olive oil in a large sauté pan over high heat. Add the bell peppers and scallions and cook, stirring, until brown, 3 to 4 minutes. Add the hearts of palm chunks, 2 teaspoons of the curry powder, and ½ teaspoon of the salt. Cook for 2 to 3 minutes, stirring occasionally to prevent burning, then transfer the mixture to a large bowl and let cool. Pulse the mixture in a food processor to achieve a coarse, shredded consistency. Set aside.

2. Preheat the oven to 400°F.

3. Heat the remaining 1 tablespoon olive oil in a large saucepan over high heat. When the oil begins to ripple, add the onions and cook, stirring, until brown, 3 to 5 minutes. Add the remaining 2 teaspoons curry powder and cook for an additional 2 to 3 minutes. Add the stock and lentils. Bring to a boil, reduce the heat, and simmer until the lentils are tender, 12 to 15 minutes. Stir in the remaining ½ teaspoon salt and the cilantro. Remove from the heat and cover to keep warm.

4. Fold the vegan mayo into the cooled hearts of palm mixture. Form the mixture into four balls. Transfer the balls to a sheet pan, flatten them into round cakes about 2 inches thick, and bake until the edges turn brown, 6 to 8 minutes.

5. To serve, spoon the lentils onto four plates and place one hearts of palm cake on top of each portion.

yukon gold potato pierogies with charred onion

PREP TIME: 45 MINUTES

COOK TIME: 55 MINUTES

SERVES 4 TO 6

2 cups all-purpose flour, plus more for dusting

5 teaspoons salt

3 tablespoons vegan butter

2 tablespoons vegan shortening

6 tablespoons olive oil, plus more for brushing

2 cups peeled, chopped Yukon Gold potatoes

1/3 cup vegan sour cream

2 teaspoons freshly ground black pepper

2 cups sliced onions

1 tablespoon apple cider vinegar

I thought I had had a pierogi before. Then, a couple of months after we started dating, Kate made me these pockets of Polish perfection that brought tears to my eyes when I ate them. We have jazzed up this recipe a bit with some smoky charred onion, but the base recipe is true to Kate's family's original. Make sure to have some extra vegan sour cream on hand when serving.

1. Make the pierogi dough by combining the flour, 3 teaspoons of the salt, 2 tablespoons of the vegan butter, and the vegan shortening in a food processor. Pulse until sandy in consistency. Add 2 tablespoons of the olive oil and continue pulsing while streaming in 4 to 6 tablespoons cold water—use just enough for the dough to come together in a soft ball. Wrap the dough in plastic wrap and refrigerate until ready to use, up to 2 days.

2. Meanwhile, bring a medium pot of salted water to a boil over high heat. Boil the potatoes until fork-tender, 10 to 12 minutes. Drain, reserving 1/4 cup of the cooking water. Transfer the potatoes back to the pot and mash with a potato masher. Stir in the vegan sour cream, reserved cooking water, remaining tablespoon of vegan butter, 1 teaspoon of the salt, and 1 teaspoon of the pepper. Set aside.

3. Roll out the dough on a work surface dusted with flour to about 1/4 inch thick. Use a 4-inch-wide circle cutter to stamp out the pierogies. Place about 2 tablespoons of the potato mixture in the center of each dough circle. Bring the edges of the circle together, forming a half circle, and pinch them together tightly. Use a fork to crimp the edges of the seal. Repeat the rolling, stamping, and filling process with the remaining scraps of dough. This process should yield about 18 pierogles.

(RECIPE CONTINUES)

4. Line a sheet pan with parchment paper and brush it lightly with olive oil. Bring a large pot of salted water to a boil over high heat. Drop four to six pierogies into the water at a time and let them boil just until they rise to the surface, about 3 minutes. Using a slotted spoon, remove them from the water and transfer them to the prepared sheet pan. Set aside.

5. Preheat the oven to 400°F.

6. Heat 2 tablespoons of the olive oil in a large sauté pan over high heat. When it begins to ripple, add the onions and the remaining 1 teaspoon salt and 1 teaspoon pepper. Reduce the heat to medium and cook, stirring, until the onions start to caramelize and become very soft, 6 to 8 minutes. Add the vinegar and cook for another 4 minutes. Transfer the mixture to a second sheet pan and bake until the edges of the onions start to turn dark brown, 10 to 12 minutes.

7. Heat the remaining 2 tablespoons oil in another large sauté pan over high heat. When it begins to ripple, add four pierogies at a time to brown on one side, then the other, 3 to 4 minutes total. Repeat until all of the pierogies are seared. Arrange the pierogies on a serving dish, top with the charred onions, and serve.

tip: An unlikely territory for vegetable-based dishes, an Eastern European–themed menu is a hearty welcome to winter around the holidays. Start the meal off with an Alpine Sensation (page 218) and the Kohlrabi Salad with White Beans and Horseradish (page 38). For a second course, bring out the Salt-Roasted Golden Beets with Dill, Avocado, Capers, and Red Onion (page 45) and the Yukon Gold Pierogies with Charred Onion. Your guests won't be able to resist trying a few Spiced Little Carrots with Chickpea-Sauerkraut Puree (page 49).

celery root fritters and rémoulade

PREP TIME: 20 MINUTES

COOK TIME: 20 MINUTES

SERVES 2 TO 4

2 cups peeled, diced celery root (about 1 pound)

½ cup chopped onions

2½ tablespoons olive oil

2 teaspoons salt

2 teaspoons freshly ground black pepper

½ cup chickpea flour (see Tip)

2 teaspoons Old Bay Seasoning

2 cups peeled, grated celery root (about 1 pound)

½ cup vegan mayo

4 cornichons

2 tablespoons capers, drained

2 tablespoons chopped fresh dill

2 tablespoons Dijon mustard

2 tablespoons coarsely chopped shallots

1 tablespoon fresh tarragon leaves

¼ cup canola oil for frying

Grand Case, on the French side of the island of St. Martin, has not just the best food in the West Indies but some of the best food we've had in the world. Even local markets carry top-notch ingredients. That's where we reunite with one of our favorite French "fast food" items: little containers of celery root rémoulade. Rémoulade is a classic French mayonnaise-based sauce similar to tartar sauce that incorporates capers, cornichons, and herbs; you won't miss a beat here by using vegan mayo. Here I've paired it with crispy, pan-fried celery root fritters that may instantly recall a crab cake or even fish and chips. The two preparations taste so different it's hard to believe you started with the same vegetable, but they complement each other beautifully.

1. Preheat the oven to 350°F.

2. Toss the diced celery root and onions in a medium bowl with 1½ tablespoons of the olive oil, 1 teaspoon of the salt, and 1 teaspoon of the pepper. Transfer the vegetables to a sheet pan and bake until the celery root is fork-tender, 12 to 15 minutes. Remove from the oven and allow to cool.

3. When fully cool, transfer the roasted celery root and onions to a food processor and pulse just until it reaches a chunky paste-like consistency. Transfer the paste to a small bowl.

4. Line a plate with parchment paper. Combine the chickpea flour and the Old Bay in another small bowl. Form each fritter by scooping one-quarter of the celery root mixture into a small ball, then flattening it out to a cake about 1½ inches thick. Dredge the fritter evenly in the chickpea flour. Set the fritter aside on the parchment-lined plate and repeat with the remaining three fritters.

(RECIPE CONTINUES)

5. Bring a large pot of salted water to a boil over high heat. Add the grated celery root to the boiling water and blanch just until it is tender while still retaining a bit of crunch, about 5 minutes. Drain and allow the celery root to cool in the colander.

6. Meanwhile, to make the rémoulade, combine the vegan mayo, cornichons, capers, dill, mustard, shallots, tarragon, ¼ cup water, and remaining 1 teaspoon salt and 1 teaspoon pepper in a food processor. Pulse until the mixture reaches a chunky but creamy consistency. Transfer to a medium bowl and fold in the cooled grated celery root.

7. Heat the canola oil in a large skillet over high heat until it starts to ripple. Carefully brown the fritters on one side, about 2 minutes, then carefully turn and brown on the other side, about 1 minute. Serve immediately on top of a scoop of rémoulade.

tip: Chickpea flour is a great alternative to traditional flour. Not only does it add flavor, it's also gluten-free.

grilled leek salad with black lentils

PREP TIME: 20 MINUTES

COOK TIME: 40 MINUTES

SERVES 6 TO 8

2 large leeks, leaves removed, cut in half lengthwise with the root still attached, rinsed well

2 tablespoons olive oil

3 teaspoons salt

2 teaspoons freshly ground black pepper

½ cup loosely packed fresh cilantro leaves

1 tablespoon sherry vinegar

1 cup finely chopped onions

½ cup finely chopped green bell peppers

4 cups Vegetable Stock (page 16)

2 cups dried black lentils, picked through and rinsed

2 teaspoons ground cumin

2 teaspoons smoked paprika

When traveling through Europe, it's hard not to notice how often leeks take the spotlight in food cultures, from Spain to Holland and everywhere in between. More than just another onion, leeks are full of their own unique flavor. They are also, however, full of dirt. It is crucial to pull them open a bit and run them under water to clean them thoroughly. In this dish, the visual contrast between the black lentils and the bright green leek salad is stunning, and the textural contrast is even better. (If you can't find black lentils, green lentils will taste just as good.)

1. Bring a large pot of salted water to a boil over high heat and prepare an ice bath. Add the leeks to the boiling water and blanch for 2 to 3 minutes. Drain the leeks, shock in the ice bath for 5 minutes, then drain thoroughly.

2. Brush the leeks with 1 tablespoon of the olive oil, then sprinkle with 1½ teaspoons of the salt and 1 teaspoon of the pepper.

3. Heat a grill pan over high heat and grill the leeks until they turn a nice, dark color, being careful not to let them burn, 5 to 7 minutes, turning them halfway. If using an outdoor grill, set it for high heat and grill the leeks for 3 to 5 minutes, turning them halfway. Set aside the leeks at room temperature until cool to the touch.

4. Discard the roots of the leeks and slice the remaining leeks crosswise into very thin slivers, no more than ⅛ inch thick, then toss them in a large bowl with the cilantro and sherry vinegar.

5. Heat the remaining 1 tablespoon oil in a medium stockpot over high heat. When it begins to ripple, add the onions and bell peppers. Cook, stirring, until brown, 5 minutes, then add the Vegetable Stock, lentils, cumin, and smoked paprika. Reduce the heat to medium-low and simmer until the lentils are tender, 25 to 30 minutes.

(RECIPE CONTINUES)

6. Stir in the remaining 1½ teaspoons salt and 1 teaspoon pepper. Spoon the lentils into serving bowls and top with the leek salad before serving.

tip: A grill pan on the stovetop can't replicate the flavor and effect of charcoal grilling, but it is the next best thing.

tarts

TARTS REPRESENT a cross between the world of savory cooking and pastries. The tart shell is rooted in the basics of good pastry technique, where fats combine to achieve a buttery flavor and flaky texture. We always recommend keeping temperatures low to preserve these qualities. In these recipes, we offer suggestions for individual-sized tarts as well as larger tarts for a more dramatic presentation. Either way, they can be served casually for personal consumption or dressed up for a dinner party, and in this way make a wonderful addition to your culinary repertoire. Feel free to adjust the fillings based on seasonal ingredients and your own personal whims.

olive and onion mini tarts

PREP TIME: 30 MINUTES

COOK TIME: 1 HOUR

SERVES 8 TO 12

TART SHELL AND FILLING

1 cup all-purpose flour, plus more for dusting

4 teaspoons salt

1 tablespoon vegan butter, cold

1 tablespoon vegan shortening, cold

4½ tablespoons olive oil

2 onions, sliced very thin

½ teaspoon freshly ground black pepper

8 ounces extra-firm tofu, drained and crumbled into small pieces

2 tablespoons balsamic vinegar

TAPENADE

½ cup pitted Niçoise olives

1 garlic clove

1½ tablespoons olive oil

1 tablespoon fresh tarragon leaves

1 tablespoon fresh thyme leaves

2 teaspoons freshly ground black pepper

When it comes to tarts and pastries, you have to take your hat off to the French. They don't mess around. On the French island of Corsica, in the town of Propriano, we found a small *boulangerie* where we had our first taste of *pissaladière*, the inspiration for this dish. Rich but not in the least bit greasy, with a wisp of fresh herbs and onions as sweet as candy, these simple French tarts will blow your mind. We've added crushed tofu for texture and body, but leave it out if you're a purist.

1. To make the tart shell dough, combine the flour and 2 teaspoons of the salt in a large bowl. Using a pastry cutter or metal fork, cut in the cold vegan butter and cold vegan shortening. Add 1 tablespoon of the olive oil and continue cutting, until the mixture is sandy in consistency. Add 2 to 3 tablespoons cold water, a little at a time, just enough to hold the dough together. Form the dough into a soft ball, wrap it in plastic wrap and refrigerate for 10 minutes or until ready to use, up to 2 days.

2. For the filling, heat 2 tablespoons of the olive oil in a large sauté pan over high heat. When it begins to ripple, add the onions, the remaining 2 teaspoons salt, and the pepper. Cook the onions, stirring as necessary, until brown, 5 to 7 minutes. Add the crumbled tofu and vinegar, then lower the heat to medium-low. Continue cooking the onions for 20 to 30 minutes. The vinegar will completely reduce.

3. Preheat the oven to 350°F. Brush the cups of a muffin pan with the remaining 1½ tablespoons olive oil.

4. On a work surface dusted with flour, roll out the tart shell dough to about ¼ inch thick. Using a circle cutter, cut the dough into rounds that are about 2 inches wider than the top of the muffin cups. Place a round of dough into each cup, pressing it into place. The dough should come about halfway up the sides of the cup. Bake the tart shells for 10 minutes, then remove from the oven.

(RECIPE CONTINUES)

5. While the tart shells are baking, make the tapenade by combining the olives, garlic, olive oil, tarragon, thyme, pepper, and 1 tablespoon water in a food processor. Puree until smooth. Set aside.

6. Divide the onion mixture evenly among the tart shells. Return to the oven and bake until the top edges of the tart shells are golden brown, 14 to 16 minutes.

7. Dollop a small spoonful of tapenade on each tart. Serve warm or at room temperature.

potato and spring vegetable tart

PREP TIME: 30 MINUTES

COOK TIME: 30 MINUTES

SERVES 6 TO 8

1 cup all-purpose flour, plus more for dusting

3 teaspoons salt

1 tablespoon vegan butter, cold

1 tablespoon vegan shortening, cold

3 tablespoons olive oil

2 cups shelled English peas

4 ounces arugula

2 cups peeled, diced Yukon gold potatoes

1 cup thinly sliced leeks

½ teaspoon freshly ground pepper

2 tablespoons chopped fresh tarragon

1 tablespoon freshly squeezed lemon juice

1 cup vegan mayo

1 tablespoon Dijon mustard

We have strong seasonal traditions and rituals when it comes to food. No summer is complete without a tequila-drenched blowout Mexican fajita party and a good old veggie BBQ. Before the holidays we seek out Eastern European and German comfort foods. In late fall you'll find us in the pub or at a country inn. But in spring, our hearts belong to the French countryside. In the Alsatian town of Colmar near the German border we had a meal whose most remarkable element was the chef's "kids' vegetable plate"—an extravaganza of chanterelle mushrooms, carrots, and snow peas, and a potato and spinach galette. All for a two-year-old . . . leave it to the French!

1. Preheat the oven to 350°F.

2. To make the dough, combine the flour and 2 teaspoons of the salt in a large bowl. Using a pastry cutter or metal fork, cut in the cold vegan butter and cold vegan shortening. Add 1 tablespoon of the olive oil and continue cutting, until the mixture is sandy in consistency. Add 2 to 3 tablespoons cold water, a little at a time, just enough to hold the dough together. Form the dough into a soft ball, wrap it in plastic wrap and refrigerate for 10 minutes or until ready to use, up to 2 days.

3. Transfer the dough to a work surface dusted with flour. Roll out the dough to about ¼ inch thick, then transfer it to an 8-inch tart pan and press it gently to fit the pan, trimming any excess. Chill for 10 minutes.

4. Bake the chilled tart shell for 6 to 8 minutes. Remove from the oven and let cool.

5. Bring a large pot of salted water to a boil over high heat and prepare an ice bath. Blanch the peas for 3 minutes, then add the arugula and allow it to slightly wilt. Drain the peas and arugula, shock them in the ice bath for 5 minutes, then drain thoroughly. Set aside.

(RECIPE CONTINUES)

6. In a medium bowl, mix the potatoes and leeks with the remaining 2 tablespoons olive oil, the remaining 1 teaspoon salt, and the pepper. Transfer to a sheet pan and bake until the potatoes are tender, 12 to 15 minutes.

7. Combine the potato mixture with the arugula mixture, the tarragon, and the lemon juice in a food processor and pulse just until the mixture sticks together (do not puree). Transfer to a large bowl and mix in the vegan mayo and mustard.

8. Fill the tart shell with the vegetable filling and bake until the tart's edge is a deep golden brown, 12 to 15 minutes. Remove the tart from the oven and let it stand for at least 20 minutes to let it set. Serve warm, or reheat to serve hot.

zucchini, tomato, and olive tart

PREP TIME: 20 MINUTES

COOK TIME: 20 MINUTES

SERVES 4 TO 6

1 cup all-purpose flour, plus more for dusting

3 teaspoons salt

1 tablespoon vegan butter, cold

1 tablespoon vegan shortening, cold

2 tablespoons olive oil

2 cups green and yellow zucchini, cut into ⅛-inch rounds (about 1⅓ pounds)

1 teaspoon freshly ground black pepper

½ cup chopped Niçoise olives

1 heirloom or other best-quality tomato, cut into six ¼-inch slices

¼ cup chopped fresh basil

This savory tart featuring summer vegetables is dedicated to the amazing restaurant Xopana at the Choupana Hills Resort in the mountains of Madeira. Most of the restaurants on the island serve traditional Portuguese cuisine, but at Xopana the chef uses seasonal and local ingredients from around this lush, beautiful garden of an island. We just so happened to be there in late July, when zucchini, tomato, and basil were all over the menu.

1. Preheat the oven to 350°F.

2. To make the dough, combine the flour and 2 teaspoons of the salt in a large bowl. Using a pastry cutter or metal fork, cut in the cold vegan butter and cold vegan shortening. Add 1 tablespoon of the olive oil and continue cutting, until the mixture is sandy in consistency. Add 2 to 3 tablespoons cold water, a little at a time, just enough to hold the dough together. Form the dough into a soft ball, wrap it in plastic wrap and refrigerate for 10 minutes or until ready to use, up to 2 days.

3. Transfer the dough to a work surface dusted with flour. Roll out the dough to about ¼ inch thick, then transfer it to an 8-inch tart pan and press it gently to fit the pan, trimming away any excess.

4. Bake the tart shell for 6 to 8 minutes, until the shell is light golden brown. Remove from the oven and let cool.

5. In a medium bowl, toss the zucchini rounds with the remaining 1 tablespoon olive oil, remaining 1 teaspoon salt, and the pepper.

6. Layer the zucchini rounds in the tart shell. Sprinkle with the olives, then lay the tomato slices on top. Bake for 12 to 15 minutes, until the tart's edge is a deep golden brown. Remove the tart from the oven and sprinkle with the basil. Serve hot, warm, or cold.

PREP TIME: 20 MINUTES

COOK TIME: 25 MINUTES

SERVES 4 TO 6

It may seem ironic that a vegetarian would look forward to Thanksgiving. A holiday that has become less about the message of thanks and more about the turkey. And the rest of the meal? Lots of brown and gray flour-thickened, heavy foods that put you to sleep. Let's re-think this food as a celebration of vegetables filling the table at the end of the harvest. The sage, rosemary, and the sweet roots are a feast of flavors and textures. This root stew is packed with color, infused with aromatics, and brought together by a rich-tasting broth. It will taste like Thanksgiving should . . . and please remember to give thanks.

1½ cups peeled, diced carrots

1½ cups peeled, diced celery root

1 cup peeled, diced parsnips

1 cup peeled, diced turnips or rutabagas

3 tablespoons olive oil

2 teaspoons salt

2 teaspoons freshly ground black pepper

¼ teaspoon allspice

Pinch of ground nutmeg

½ cup diced onions

2 teaspoons ground sage

½ cup dry white wine

8 cups Vegetable Stock (page 16)

2 teaspoons finely chopped fresh rosemary

1. Preheat the oven to 400°F.

2. Toss the carrots, celery root, parsnips, and turnips in a large bowl with 2 tablespoons of the oil, 1 teaspoon of the salt, 1 teaspoon of the pepper, the allspice, and nutmeg. Transfer the vegetables to a sheet pan in a single layer and roast until they are fork-tender, 12 to 15 minutes.

3. Meanwhile, heat the remaining 1 tablespoon oil in a large stock-pot over high heat until it ripples. Add the onions and sage and allow to brown, 3 to 5 minutes, stirring occasionally to prevent burning.

4. Deglaze with the wine and cook until it is reduced by half, 3 to 5 minutes.

5. Add the stock and bring to a boil. Add the roasted vegetables. Reduce the heat and simmer for 5 minutes, stirring occasionally.

6. Add the rosemary to the stew, remove the pot from the heat, and serve.

portobello and celery root shepherd's pie with truffle

PREP TIME: 30 MINUTES

COOK TIME: 35 MINUTES

SERVES 4

5 medium portobellos, stems reserved, caps wiped clean

4 tablespoons olive oil

1½ teaspoons salt

1 cup peeled, diced carrots

1 cup peeled, diced turnips

½ cup chopped onions

1 teaspoon minced garlic

1 teaspoon freshly ground black pepper

2 teaspoons Dijon mustard

2 teaspoons chopped fresh thyme

2 cups peeled, diced celery root

1 cup peeled, diced Yukon Gold potatoes

½ cup vegan sour cream

1 tablespoon white truffle oil

Shepherd's pie: what might seem pedestrian and quaint can be made chic and sophisticated. We use a whole portobello mushroom as the base and then top it with mashed celery root and potatoes spiked with truffle. There's plenty of work going into it ahead of time to give beautiful results, but the final step, heating the stuffed portobello cap, can be done just before serving.

1. Preheat the oven to 400°F.

2. Dice the portobello stems and one of the caps to match the size of the diced carrots and turnips. Set aside.

3. Using a pastry brush, apply 2 tablespoons of the olive oil to the remaining four portobello caps. Place them on a sheet pan, rounded sides up, and sprinkle with ½ teaspoon of the salt.

4. Roast the caps for 8 to 12 minutes, or until they have lost some of their water volume—you will see liquid build up outside the mushroom shell. Remove from the oven and set aside.

5. Toss the diced portobellos, carrots, turnips, onions, and garlic with the remaining 2 tablespoons olive oil, ½ teaspoon of the salt, and ½ teaspoon of the pepper. Spread the mixture on a sheet pan and roast until the carrots and turnips are fork-tender, 12 to 15 minutes.

6. Remove the roasted vegetables from the oven and toss in the mustard and thyme. Set aside.

7. Bring a medium pot of salted water to a boil over high heat. Add the celery root and potatoes and boil until fork-tender, 8 to 12 minutes.

(RECIPE CONTINUES)

8. Drain the celery root and potato, reserving ¼ cup of the cooking water. Transfer the celery root, potato, and reserved cooking water to a food processor and add the vegan sour cream, truffle oil, and the remaining ½ teaspoon salt and ½ teaspoon pepper. Pulse until smooth and creamy.

9. Turn the remaining portobello caps upside down and stuff them with the roasted diced vegetables.

10. Seal the caps by completely covering the diced vegetables with the celery root and potato puree.

11. Return the caps to the oven and bake until the puree on top starts to brown, 6 to 10 minutes. Serve immediately.

tip: From our journeys in Ireland, England, Scotland, and the British West Indies, no place on the planet says home like a cozy pub, pint in hand. This menu is a fire-lit autumn celebration of being home with comforting food. The shepherd's pie is the main course, and the Fingerling Potatoes with Creamy Worcestershire Sauce (page 80) are even better with a bowl of Hedgehog Mushroom, Turnip, and Barley Stew (page 61) and a pint of dark ale. The Figgy Toffee Pudding with Madeira-Quince Ice Cream (page 187) offers a traditional English pub ending to this meal.

royal trumpet mushroom cioppino

PREP TIME: 20 MINUTES

COOK TIME: 30 MINUTES

SERVES 4 TO 6

1 pound royal trumpet mushrooms, very bottoms of stems removed, wiped clean

4 tablespoons olive oil

1 cup finely sliced leeks, rinsed well

2 tablespoons minced garlic

1 cup finely sliced fennel, fronds removed

½ cup dry white wine

3 cups Vegetable Stock (page 16)

One 16-ounce can diced tomatoes, preferably San Marzano

1 tablespoon Old Bay Seasoning

1½ teaspoons salt

1 teaspoon freshly ground black pepper

1 tablespoon chopped fresh thyme or oregano

1 teaspoon crushed red pepper flakes

4 to 6 slices bread, such as our House Bread (page 207) or a nice sourdough, grilled or toasted

Cioppino is one of the most famous American culinary inventions, created by homesick Italians in San Francisco. The classic cioppino is a tomato-based seafood stew served over linguini or with crusty bread. For our Vedge version we feature thinly shaved royal trumpet mushrooms that add superb texture and flavor. If you can't find them, oyster mushrooms (a distant cousin of the royal trumpet) will also work well. The fennel and leek bring a green touch of spring to this stew.

1. Slice the mushrooms lengthwise as thinly as possible. A mandoline works best, or use a knife and slice really thin.

2. Heat 2 tablespoons of the olive oil in a large stockpot over high heat until it ripples. Add the leeks and garlic and cook, stirring, until brown, 3 to 5 minutes.

3. Add the sliced mushrooms and continue to brown for another 3 to 5 minutes.

4. Stir in the fennel, then the wine. Let the wine come to a boil, reduce the heat to medium, and simmer for 2 minutes.

5. Add the stock, tomatoes with their juices, Old Bay, salt, and pepper and bring to a boil. Reduce the heat to medium-low and simmer until the mushrooms are tender and the fennel is soft, about 15 minutes. Stir in the thyme and crushed red pepper flakes.

6. Ladle the soup into bowls. Drizzle with the remaining 2 tablespoons olive oil and garnish with the bread.

whole roasted carrots with black lentils and green *harissa*

PREP TIME: 20 MINUTES

COOK TIME: 55 MINUTES

SERVES 4 TO 6

CARROTS

2 pounds jumbo carrots, washed well

2 tablespoons olive oil

2 tablespoons Island Spice Blend (page 20)

LENTILS

1 tablespoon olive oil

½ cup minced onions

1 tablespoon minced garlic

3 cups Vegetable Stock (page 16)

2 cups dried black or green lentils, picked through and rinsed

2 teaspoons Island Spice Blend (page 20)

Around Thanksgiving, the press loves to ask, "What do you people do?" Well, in our house, we don't do just sides—we always pick a grand centerpiece. Be it portobellos, giant squash, tender eggplants, or whole roasted jumbo carrots, I love putting giant chunks of vegetables center plate. When perfectly cooked, the knife-and-fork eating experience of these carrots is unmatched. Their creamy, rich texture is a perfect contrast to the toothsome lentils. And the green *harissa*, our take on the classic Tunisian hot sauce, adds a tangy high note that contrasts the sweetness and earthiness. Buy jumbo carrots loose or, if buying bagged carrots, reduce the cooking time by half. If the carrots come with greens, cut them off but leave about one inch of the stem.

1. Preheat the oven to 400°F.

2. Toss the carrots on a sheet pan with the olive oil and Island Spice Blend. Roast until they just start to become tender, 15 to 20 minutes.

3. Meanwhile, to make the lentils, heat the oil in a medium stockpot over high heat until it ripples. Add the minced onions and garlic and cook, stirring, until brown, 3 to 5 minutes. Add the stock, lentils, and Island Spice Blend and bring to a boil. Reduce the heat to medium-low and simmer, uncovered, until the lentils are tender, 25 to 30 minutes.

(INGREDIENTS CONTINUE)

(RECIPE CONTINUES)

4. Meanwhile, combine all of the harissa ingredients in a blender and blend until smooth.

5. To serve, spoon the lentils onto a serving dish, place the roasted carrots on top of the lentils, and cover the carrots with the harissa.

2 cups loosely packed fresh cilantro leaves

1 cup chopped onions

2 garlic cloves

2 jalapeño peppers, stems and seeds removed

2 tablespoons olive oil

2 tablespoons rice wine vinegar

1 teaspoon ground coriander

1 teaspoon ground cumin

1 teaspoon salt

1 teaspoon freshly ground black pepper

1 teaspoon sugar

I could spend hours wandering the side streets of Paris, popping into cafés with their inviting little patios adorned with pots of flowers and ornate signage. Unfortunately, I could spend very few of those hours actually eating, so I am constantly drawn to reimagining animal-free versions of French classics. This is one of our favorite go-to dishes for special-occasion menus at Vedge. For the elegant results, this dish is relatively easy to prepare, and its herbed red wine and mushroom *jus* will whisk you right off to that Parisian corner café. If you can't find *maitakes*, oyster mushrooms will also work well. In the dish that we photographed, we took a standard turnip, cut it into a medallion, and roasted it just like the quartered or halved turnips in this recipe.

1. Preheat the oven to 450°F.

2. Break or cut the mushrooms into 3- to 4-inch chunks. Toss the mushroom chunks, turnips, carrots, onions, olive oil, garlic, salt, and pepper in a large bowl. Pour the mixture into a 13 x 9-inch casserole dish and bake for 10 minutes.

3. Pour the wine over the roasted vegetables, stir, then cover the dish with foil or a lid and bake for an additional 10 minutes.

4. Remove the foil and pour the vegetable stock over the vegetables. Return the dish to the oven, uncovered, for 10 more minutes. Add the thyme and stir gently, then serve.

PREP TIME: 20 MINUTES

COOK TIME: 30 MINUTES

SERVES 4

2 pounds maitake, bottoms of stems removed, caps wiped clean

1 pound baby turnips, halved, *or* standard turnips, quartered

1 carrot, peeled and sliced into ¼-inch rounds

1 cup diced onions

¼ cup olive oil

2 tablespoons minced garlic

1 teaspoon salt

1 teaspoon freshly ground black pepper

2 cups dry red wine

2 cups Vegetable Stock (page 16)

1 tablespoon chopped fresh thyme

portobello frites

PREP TIME: 20 MINUTES
COOK TIME: 1 HOUR
SERVES 4

2 russet potatoes, scrubbed

1 teaspoon coarse sea salt

¼ cup olive oil

2 teaspoons salt

1 teaspoon minced garlic

1 teaspoon freshly ground black pepper

1 teaspoon minced shallots

4 portobello mushrooms, stems removed, caps wiped clean (see Tip)

1 cup dry red wine

¼ cup Vegetable Stock (page 16)

1 teaspoon Dijon mustard

1 tablespoon chopped fresh tarragon

¼ cup canola oil for frying

Like most Francophiles, when we are not traveling to French-speaking (and -eating) destinations, we are at home, dreaming of them and inspired by them as we cook the foods we love. Steak frites is the definitive French bistro dish; our portobello version features a juicy red wine reduction that sings with tarragon and a touch of Dijon. You can easily make restaurant-crisp fries at home with the Vedge method: start with baked potatoes, then crisp them up in a little oil.

1. Preheat the oven to 400°F. Puncture each potato with a fork three times, sprinkle each with ½ teaspoon of the coarse sea salt, and wrap individually in foil. Bake until tender to the touch, about 40 minutes. Unwrap the potatoes and let cool; when cool enough to handle, cut each into eight wedges. Set aside.

2. While the potatoes are cooling, whisk together the olive oil, 1 teaspoon of the salt, the garlic, pepper, and shallots in a small bowl.

3. Place the portobello caps on a sheet pan with rimmed edges and coat them evenly on both sides with the olive oil mixture, leaving them rounded sides up. Roast until soft in the middle, 8 to 12 minutes.

4. Transfer the portobello caps to a plate, still rounded sides up, and set aside to cool. Pour the wine, vegetable stock, and mustard onto the warm sheet pan to mix with the mushroom cooking juices. Scrape any solids off the tray, then carefully pour this mixture into a large saucepan. Heat the mixture over medium heat until reduced by half, 8 to 10 minutes.

(RECIPE CONTINUES)

5. Stir the tarragon into the red wine sauce. Remove the saucepan from the heat and cover to keep warm.

6. In a large sauté pan, heat the canola oil over high heat. When the oil is very hot, carefully fry a few potato wedges at a time until they turn brown on all sides, about 6 minutes. Transfer the frites as they are done to a plate lined with paper towels and sprinkle them lightly with the remaining 1 teaspoon salt.

7. Reheat the portobello caps in the oven if necessary. Serve smothered with red wine sauce and frites on the side.

tip: Save the portobello stems for Portobello Stem *Anti-cuchos* (page 39).

royal trumpet mushroom "blt" with basil mayo

PREP TIME: 10 MINUTES

COOK TIME: 20 MINUTES

SERVES 2

½ pound royal trumpet mushrooms, very bottoms of stems removed, wiped clean

2 tablespoons olive oil

1 teaspoon salt

1 teaspoon freshly ground black pepper

¼ cup vegan mayo

2 tablespoons finely chopped basil

4 slices House Bread, toasted (page 207)

1 cup shredded romaine lettuce

1 tomato, sliced and sprinkled lightly with salt and pepper

Royal trumpet mushrooms are one of my favorite ingredients. Big, meaty tubes of usable flesh, they are easy to work with and offer a pleasantly chewy texture. When cooked properly, royal trumpets can fit well into nearly any recipe that calls for mushrooms. Slice them thickly crosswise and you have "scallops" to sear in a pan. Roast them whole in the oven with herbs and olive oil and serve over mashed potatoes for a "meat and potatoes" fix. But my favorite preparation is slicing them into very thin planks and frying them up like bacon. As a sandwich, this is an easy crowd pleaser. For a cocktail party, serve open-face on crostini.

1. Slice the mushrooms lengthwise into very thin planks. Heat the olive oil in a large skillet over high heat. When it starts to ripple, arrange a single layer of mushroom slices in the pan and sear until brown and crispy, 2½ to 3 minutes on each side. Transfer to a plate lined with paper towels. Repeat this process until all mushrooms are seared. Sprinkle the mushrooms with ½ teaspoon of the salt and ½ teaspoon of the pepper.

2. Meanwhile, whisk the vegan mayo, basil, and remaining ½ teaspoon salt and ½ teaspoon pepper in a small bowl until the basil is evenly incorporated.

3. To assemble the sandwiches, spread the mayo on the bread slices. Pile the romaine, mushrooms, and tomatoes on two slices, cover with the top slices of basil mayo–slathered bread, and serve.

fazzoletti with peas and morels

PREP TIME: 30 MINUTES

COOK TIME: 30 MINUTES

SERVES 2 TO 4

1 cup semolina flour

1½ teaspoons salt

2 cups shelled English peas

2 tablespoons olive oil

2 tablespoons minced shallots

½ pound morel mushrooms, very bottoms of stems removed, wiped clean and sliced thin

1 teaspoon freshly ground black pepper

¼ cup dry white wine

½ cup Vegetable Stock (page 16)

1 teaspoon chopped fresh tarragon

1 teaspoon chopped fresh thyme

Like most people, I love pasta, but I'm still dismayed when the only vegetarian offering on a restaurant's otherwise creative menu is the dreaded token pasta. This dish is mainly a celebration of spring vegetables—it just happens to include a stellar fresh pasta. Semolina flour gives it a nice, punchy resistance on the palate. Keep an eye on the cooking time—when it floats to the top, it's done. The classic springtime combination of fresh peas and morel mushrooms is timeless, but feel free to substitute any fresh beans (such as favas) or mushrooms.

1. Line a sheet pan with parchment paper and set aside. Sift together the semolina flour and 1 teaspoon of the salt in a large bowl. Drizzle in 1 cup water and knead to make a dough. Let the dough rest for 5 minutes, then use a pasta roller or rolling pin to roll it out as thin as possible—you should have a rectangle approximately 12 inches by 15 inches. Use a knife to cut the dough into twenty 3-inch squares. Place the squares on the prepared sheet pan, cover with plastic wrap, and set aside at room temperature until ready to use.

2. Bring a large pot of salted water to a boil over high heat. Blanch the peas for 4 to 5 minutes, then use a slotted spoon to transfer them to a bowl. Set the peas aside to cool at room temperature. Leave the water boiling.

(RECIPE CONTINUES)

3. Heat the olive oil in a large sauté pan over high heat. When the oil starts to ripple, add the shallots and cook, stirring, until brown, 3 to 5 minutes. Add the morels, pepper, and remaining ½ teaspoon salt and cook, stirring, until brown, 3 to 5 more minutes. Deglaze with the wine and reduce by half, 3 to 5 minutes. Add the Vegetable Stock and peas.

4. Slowly drop all of the pasta squares into the boiling water. After 2 to 3 minutes, as each square floats to the surface, remove it with a slotted spoon and transfer to a holding plate until all of the pasta is cooked.

5. Reduce the heat on the sauté pan to medium low. Add the pasta to the sauce with the tarragon and thyme and stir, allowing it to absorb some of the flavors of the sauce, 3 to 4 minutes. Serve immediately.

tip: Morels can be found at specialty markets or online. Morels are very porous and always trap dirt, so even if they look clean they still need to be soaked.

lentil haggis with neeps and tatties

PREP TIME: 15 MINUTES

COOK TIME: 35 MINUTES

SERVES 2 TO 4

HAGGIS

2 cups cooked lentils *or* one 15-ounce can lentils, rinsed and drained

½ cup fresh bread crumbs

1 tablespoon olive oil, plus more for brushing

1 tablespoon chopped onions

1 teaspoon chopped garlic

1 teaspoon ground sage

1 teaspoon salt

1 teaspoon freshly ground black pepper

½ teaspoon ground cumin

¼ teaspoon ground cloves

¼ teaspoon ground nutmeg

NEEPS AND TATTIES

1 pound fingerling potatoes

2 tablespoons olive oil

2 teaspoons salt

2 teaspoons freshly ground black pepper

½ cup beer, preferably Samuel Smith's Pale Ale

2 large turnips, peeled and cut into ½-inch dice (about 2 pounds)

1 teaspoon sugar

2 tablespoons vegan sour cream

The surprisingly large vegetarian population throughout the UK allows for liberal interpretations of some of the most classic British dishes. Here, Scottish haggis is reworked with lentils for the vegetarian kitchen and served with the traditional "neeps and tatties" (turnips and potatoes). Kate and I make it a mission to seek out vegetarian versions of local specialties when we travel. We struck gold on a Christmas Eve visit to Edinburgh, Scotland when we found this dish in a restaurant on the Royal Mile.

1. Preheat the oven to 350°F.

2. Combine all of the haggis ingredients in a food processor. Pulse until the lentils are broken down and all the ingredients are well incorporated.

3. Brush a sheet pan lightly with olive oil. Form the lentil mixture into a loaf and place in the center of the sheet pan. Bake until browned and firm to the touch, 10 to 12 minutes.

4. To make the "tatties," toss the fingerling potatoes in a medium bowl with the olive oil, 1 teaspoon of the salt, and 1 teaspoon of the pepper. Transfer to a sheet pan and bake until tender, 12 to 15 minutes.

5. Meanwhile, to make the "neeps," bring a large stockpot of salted water to a boil over high heat. Add the beer to the water and boil the turnips until tender, 6 to 8 minutes. Reserve ½ cup of the boiling liquid, then drain the turnips. Return them to the pot, add the reserved boiling liquid, sugar, and remaining 1 teaspoon salt and 1 teaspoon pepper. Mash the turnips with a potato masher, then fold in the vegan sour cream.

6. Serve slices of the roasted haggis with the neeps and tatties on the side.

The first wisps of cool fall weather inspire me more than any other time of the year. It's at these moments that I love to re-invent classic rustic dishes like this one, cassoulet. The traditional recipe calls for all sorts of body parts, but I skip over those in favor of the season's best roots and squashes. I was able to preserve some level of authenticity, however, when a local farmer brought me what he swore were genuine Tarbais beans. He recounted a sordid tale about the smuggling of the precious beans by a farmer friend of his to the States despite the best efforts of French law enforcement to keep them within the region of Tarbes. I personally can't vouch for their authenticity, but the beans I cooked were, indeed, unmatchable in their texture and flavor. So if you run into any gangster-farmers at the market, try to get your hands on authentic Tarbais beans. You may also be able to find them online. Otherwise, just substitute white kidney beans.

1. Preheat the oven to 400°F.

2. Toss the celery root, rutabagas, and squash in a large bowl with the onions, olive oil, salt, pepper, and nutmeg. Transfer the mixture to a sheet pan in a single layer and bake until the vegetables are fork-tender, about 15 minutes.

3. Remove the pan from the oven and carefully pour the wine over the roots to deglaze. Transfer the vegetables to a large bowl and fold in the beans.

4. Whisk together the stock, thyme, tomato paste, and sage in a small saucepan over high heat. As soon as it comes to a boil, pour it over the roasted vegetable mixture.

5. Divide the cassoulet among individual gratin dishes or transfer to one large casserole dish. Bake for 5 to 10 minutes to heat through, then serve.

winter vegetable cassoulet

PREP TIME: 20 MINUTES

COOK TIME: 30 MINUTES

SERVES 4 TO 6

2 cups peeled, ¼-inch-diced celery root (1½ pounds)

2 cups peeled, ¼-inch-diced rutabaga (1½ pounds)

1 cup peeled, ½-inch-diced winter squash, such as butternut or acorn (about ½ pound)

¼ cup finely chopped onions

2 tablespoons olive oil

1 teaspoon salt

1 teaspoon freshly ground black pepper

¼ teaspoon ground nutmeg

¼ cup dry white wine

3 cups cooked white beans *or* two 15-ounce cans white beans, rinsed and drained

1 cup Mushroom Stock (page 17) or Vegetable Stock (page 16)

2 teaspoons chopped fresh thyme

2 teaspoons tomato paste

1 teaspoon chopped fresh sage

eggplant braciole

PREP TIME: 45 MINUTES

COOK TIME: 30 MINUTES

SERVES 4 TO 6

The braciole is one of our signature dishes at Vedge and one of my personal favorites. I hesitated to include it here since it's also the most involved and labor intensive dish we make. However, after some experimentation, we hit on a great compromise with this home kitchen version. It's still a good amount of work, but the results are really impressive. You want the eggplant sheets to be as close to paper thin as possible; this is the recipe to invest in a mandoline for if you haven't already. A traditional Italian salsa verde is based around fresh herbs, garlic, capers, and anchovies—about as far from the tomatillo-based Mexican version as you can get. We add lemon juice and thin it out with vegetable stock to make a fresh green statement on the plate.

8 tablespoons olive oil

2 teaspoons balsamic vinegar

1½ teaspoons salt

1½ teaspoons freshly ground black pepper

1 large eggplant, sliced lengthwise on a mandoline into very thin sheets, ends reserved

1 head cauliflower, leaves and stem removed

½ cup cooked white rice

1 cup firmly packed fresh basil leaves

1 cup firmly packed baby spinach leaves

½ cup Vegetable Stock (page 16)

1 garlic clove

1 tablespoon capers, drained

1 tablespoon freshly squeezed lemon juice

1. Preheat the oven to 400°F.

2. Combine 3 tablespoons of the olive oil in a small bowl with the balsamic vinegar, ½ teaspoon of the salt, and ½ teaspoon of the pepper. Place the eggplant slices on a sheet pan in a single layer, using multiple pans if necessary, and brush both sides with the marinade. Roast until the eggplant becomes translucent, 4 to 5 minutes, being very careful not to let the edges burn. Remove from the oven and set aside to cool.

3. Chop the cauliflower and ends of the eggplant into 1-inch chunks. Transfer to a large bowl and toss with 3 tablespoons of the olive oil, ½ teaspoon of the salt, and ½ teaspoon of the pepper. Spread out the vegetables on a sheet pan and roast until tender, 12 to 15 minutes. Remove from the oven and transfer to a food processor. Pulse to a rice-like consistency. Transfer the mixture to a medium bowl and fold in the cooked rice.

(RECIPE CONTINUES)

4. Assemble the braciole by laying two eggplant slices on a cutting board so that the long edges overlap each other a bit, forming one large rectangle. Spoon about ½ cup of the cauliflower mixture lengthwise down the center seam where the edges overlap. Beginning with a short side of the rectangle, wrap the eggplant slices around the filling by rolling over the mixture. You should end up with four to six braciole, depending on the number of eggplant slices. Place the braciole on a sheet pan and roast until golden brown, 7 to 9 minutes.

5. Meanwhile, make the salsa verde by combining the basil, spinach, Vegetable Stock, garlic, capers, lemon juice, and remaining 2 tablespoons olive oil, ½ teaspoon salt, and ½ teaspoon pepper in a clean food processor. Pulse to a pesto-like consistency.

6. Transfer the salsa verde to a small saucepan and heat over low heat just until it turns bright green, 2 to 3 minutes. Remove from the heat.

7. Top the braciole with the warm salsa verde and serve.

baked potato *poutine* with porcini gravy

PREP TIME: 10 MINUTES

COOK TIME: 1 HOUR 10 MINUTES

SERVES 4

2 russet potatoes, scrubbed

1 teaspoon coarse sea salt

2 tablespoons plus 1 teaspoon olive oil

1 teaspoon salt

½ teaspoon freshly ground black pepper

2 tablespoons all-purpose flour

2 tablespoons canola oil

2 cups Mushroom Stock (page 17)

1 tablespoon porcini powder

¼ cup vegan sour cream

2 teaspoons Montreal Steak Spice Blend (page 20)

1 cup drained, diced extra-firm tofu

In search of poutine . . . We land in Montreal and drive to the nearest boulangerie to load up on provisions, crusty baguettes, tapenade, piperade, wine, and prepared vegetables. We drive Northwest, and about an hour later we are in a little slice of France, Canadian style: Mont Tremblant. We fell in love with this (somewhat contrived) ski resort village. There, we found one of our favorite restaurants, La Petite Cachée. And, happily, we found poutine—a vegetarian version, nonetheless, that we adored. (The original is a heart attack of fries with beef gravy and cheese curds.) Still not a dish you want to eat every day, our version takes a lighter approach—baking instead of frying the potatoes—and it's ideal for sharing.

1. Preheat the oven to 400°F. Puncture each potato with a fork three times, sprinkle each with ½ teaspoon coarse sea salt, and wrap individually in foil. Bake until tender to the touch, about 40 minutes. Unwrap the potatoes and let cool; when cool enough to handle, cut each into eight wedges.

2. Arrange the potato wedges on a sheet pan. Brush them with 2 tablespoons of the olive oil, then sprinkle with ½ teaspoon of the salt and ¼ teaspoon of the pepper. Bake until golden and slightly crispy, 10 to 12 minutes.

3. Meanwhile, prepare the gravy by cooking the flour and canola oil together in a medium sauté pan over medium heat, whisking often until it turns light brown, 4 to 6 minutes. Slowly add the Mushroom Stock, porcini powder, and remaining ½ teaspoon salt and ¼ teaspoon pepper, whisking continuously to prevent clumping. Bring the gravy to a simmer and then remove from the heat. Cover to keep warm.

4. Whisk the vegan sour cream in a small bowl with 1 tablespoon water, the remaining 1 teaspoon olive oil, and the steak spice blend. Fold in the tofu, then transfer the mixture to a sheet pan and bake until the sour cream sticks to and coats the tofu, 8 to 10 minutes. Remove from the oven and allow to cool for 5 minutes.

5. Arrange the potato wedges on a serving dish, smother with gravy, then crumble the tofu on top and serve.

squash empanadas with green *romesco*

PREP TIME: 30 MINUTES

COOK TIME: 30 MINUTES

SERVES 2 TO 4

1 cup all-purpose flour, plus more for dusting

3 teaspoons salt

1 tablespoon vegan butter, cold

1 tablespoon vegan shortening, cold

4 tablespoons olive oil

3 cups peeled, chopped calabaza squash (about 1½ pounds)

1 teaspoon freshly ground black pepper

½ teaspoon ground coriander

½ teaspoon ground cumin

1 green bell pepper, stem and seeds removed, cut into 6 chunks

1 poblano pepper, stem and seeds removed, cut into 6 chunks

2 garlic cloves

½ cup raw almonds

½ cup loosely packed fresh cilantro leaves

1 teaspoon sherry vinegar

To this day, I am haunted by the pictures in a beautiful photo book I picked up at the airport on the Spanish island of Mallorca, teasing me for all that we had missed on our short stay. Out-of-the-way beaches, rolling green countryside, and tucked-away little villages. But it was here, on the largest of the Balearic Islands, that Kate and I started our Spanish culinary journey before moving on to the mainland. We fell in love with the bold flavors, and they remain in our cooking repertoire to this day. Empanadas are a Spanish classic, enjoyed throughout Spain and much of the Latin world. We call for baking them, but go ahead and deep-fry or pan-fry them if you want. The squash we prefer is calabaza, a West Indian pumpkin, but any cold-weather, creamy-fleshed squash, such as butternut, will work. Romesco is a fiery Spanish condiment made from almonds, garlic, and red peppers. We have some fun with it here by making a green version.

1. To make the dough, combine the flour and 2 teaspoons of the salt in a large bowl. Using a pastry cutter or metal fork, cut in the cold vegan butter and cold vegan shortening. Add 1 tablespoon of the olive oil and continue cutting, until the mixture is sandy in consistency. Add 2 to 3 tablespoons cold water, a little at a time, just enough to hold the dough together. Form the dough into a soft ball, wrap it in plastic wrap and refrigerate for 10 minutes or until ready to use, up to 2 days.

2. Preheat the oven to 400°F. Line a sheet pan with parchment paper and set aside.

3. Toss the squash in a medium bowl with 2 tablespoons of the olive oil, ½ teaspoon of the salt, ½ teaspoon of the pepper, the coriander, and the cumin. Transfer to a sheet pan and roast until fork-tender, 8 to 12 minutes. Remove from the oven, return to the bowl, and, while still warm, mash with a potato masher or large spoon.

(RECIPE CONTINUES)

4. Roll out the dough on a work surface dusted with flour to about ¼ inch thick. Use a 4-inch-wide circle cutter to stamp out the empanadas. Place 1 heaping tablespoon of the squash mixture in the center of each dough circle. Bring the edges of the circle together, forming a half circle, and pinch them together tightly. Use a fork to crimp the edges of the seal. Arrange the empanadas on the prepared sheet pan.

5. Bake the empanadas until golden brown, 10 to 12 minutes.

6. Meanwhile, prepare the romesco by tossing the bell pepper and poblano pepper in another medium bowl with the garlic cloves and the remaining 1 tablespoon olive oil, ½ teaspoon salt, and ½ teaspoon pepper. Transfer to a sheet pan and roast until the peppers soften, 6 to 8 minutes. Add the almonds and roast for an additional 2 to 3 minutes. Transfer to a food processor and add the cilantro, sherry vinegar, and ½ cup water. Pulse until smooth.

7. As soon as the empanadas are done, serve them with the romesco.

In this new take on spinach pie, black kale takes the place of spinach. Also known as dinosaur, lacinato, or Tuscan kale, the leaves are dark and bumpy, and the flavor is a bit sweeter than curly kale. The tofu provides a creamy, crumbly texture that fuses the hearty greens with the delicate phyllo. Phyllo itself is surprisingly easy to work with, so don't be intimidated. The Fillo Factory is a fantastic, organic brand. Just remember to thaw it on the countertop for about a half hour before using.

1. Preheat the oven to 350°F. Brush a sheet pan lightly with olive oil. Bring a large pot of salted water to a boil over high heat.

2. Blanch the kale for 5 minutes, then drain in a colander. (Do not shock the kale in an ice bath.)

3. Heat the olive oil in a large skillet over high heat until it ripples. Add the onions and garlic and cook, stirring, until brown, 2 to 3 minutes.

4. Add the crumbled tofu, salt, and pepper. Stir the tofu around, letting it brown evenly for 8 to 10 minutes.

5. Combine the kale and the tofu mixture in a large bowl. Add the vegan sour cream, dill, and lemon juice.

6. Layer 3 to 4 sheets of phyllo on the sheet pan. Add one-third of the kale and tofu mixture. Then layer again with 3 to 4 sheets of phyllo and the next one-third of the mixture. Repeat to create a third layer of phyllo sheets and mixture, then top with a final layer of phyllo.

7. Brush the top layer of phyllo lightly with olive oil, then bake until golden brown, 12 to 15 minutes. Serve warm.

black kale as spanakopita

PREP TIME: 25 MINUTES
COOK TIME: 30 MINUTES
SERVES 6 TO 8

2 tablespoons olive oil, plus more for brushing

2 large bunches black kale, stems removed, leaves chopped (about 2 pounds)

1 cup finely chopped onions

2 teaspoons minced garlic

1 pound extra-firm tofu, drained and crumbled into small pieces

2 teaspoons salt

2 teaspoons freshly ground black pepper

1½ cups vegan sour cream

2 tablespoons chopped fresh dill

1 tablespoon freshly squeezed lemon juice

One-half of a 1-pound package vegan phyllo dough, preferably The Fillo Factory brand, thawed according to package instructions

grilled zucchini with green olives, cilantro, and tomato

PREP TIME: 10 MINUTES

COOK TIME: 10 MINUTES

SERVES 4

4 tablespoons olive oil

2 teaspoons tamari

2 teaspoons freshly ground black pepper

1 teaspoon balsamic vinegar

3 zucchini, each sliced lengthwise into 3 equal-sized planks (about 2 pounds)

1 tablespoon minced garlic

¾ cup diced tomatoes

¼ cup drained, sliced pimiento-stuffed green olives

½ teaspoon salt

¾ cup Vegetable Stock (page 16)

2 tablespoons chopped fresh cilantro

An early food inspiration from a cooking show came to me one late night as a 7th grader watching *Doctor Who* (yes, the old ones) on PBS. At the end of the show, with space to fill, they showed these 7 minute cooking segments. I remember this enormous guy in a chef's jacket cooking a steak this particular night and for the sauce he was sautéing . . . olives??? I was blown away by this idea, and it has been in my culinary repertoire ever since. Zucchini on the grill, done right, is one of the greatest summer dishes. Make sure you cut it thick enough so it doesn't collapse, and don't overcook it—let it be crunchy and bright. This sauce will recall a classic Veracruz sauce from Mexico, but its inspiration is pure summer produce and a fat chef on PBS. Thanks, dude.

1. Make the marinade by whisking 2 tablespoons of the olive oil in a small bowl with the tamari, 1 teaspoon of the pepper, and the balsamic vinegar.

2. Brush the zucchini planks on all sides with the marinade.

3. Heat a grill pan over high heat, then sear the planks of zucchini for about 2 minutes on each side, in batches if necessary. Alternatively, an outdoor grill works even better. Set it to high and char each side until you see clearly defined grill marks, 3 to 4 minutes total. Arrange the grilled planks on a serving dish.

4. Meanwhile, to make the sauce, heat the remaining 2 tablespoons olive oil in a large sauté pan over high heat. When the oil begins to ripple, add the garlic and brown for 2 to 3 minutes. Add the tomatoes, olives, salt, and remaining 1 teaspoon pepper. Continue to cook for 3 minutes, then add the stock and cook until it reduces by one-quarter, about 5 minutes. Stir in the cilantro, then pour the dressing over the grilled zucchini and serve.

korean eggplant tacos with kimchi mayo

PREP TIME: 15 MINUTES

COOK TIME: 15 MINUTES

SERVES 2 TO 4

1 tablespoon gochujang

2 teaspoons tamari

2 teaspoons rice wine vinegar

1 teaspoon sugar

2 Japanese eggplants, peeled and julienned (substitute 1 Italian eggplant, peeled and seeded, if necessary)

2 tablespoons toasted sesame oil

½ cup vegan kimchi, drained, chopped fine

1 cup vegan mayo

Four to six 6-inch flour tortillas

½ cup fresh cilantro leaves

½ cup chopped scallions, white and light green parts only

Read the food blogs from Los Angeles today and you'll glimpse what's heading east next year. When Korean tacos were all the rage in LA a few years ago I didn't wait for the trend to reach our coast. I had to try my hand at recreating this addictive street food featuring traditional Korean proteins and condiments stuffed inside Mexican tortillas. Our Philly customers were quick to appreciate the addictive harmony of spice plus funk. These tacos are now a mainstay at Vedge. You could amp up the protein by filling them with tofu or seitan, but I find that eggplant works especially well as a vehicle for the sweet gochujang glaze. If gochujang is unavailable, substitute a mixture of equal parts chili sauce and miso sauce. If necessary, you can prepare this using 1 Italian eggplant, peeled and seeded. Just make sure to cut it into very thin strips, no more than a quarter inch thick.

1. Preheat the oven to 400°F.

2. Make the glaze by whisking together the gochujang, tamari, vinegar, and sugar in a large bowl.

3. In another large bowl, toss the eggplants in the sesame oil.

4. Heat a large sauté pan over high heat. It is important to get a nice sear on the eggplant, so start by arranging the strips in a thin layer across the bottom of the pan and letting them get crisp, about 5 minutes. You may need to do this in two or more batches depending on how large your pan is. Transfer the eggplant slices to the bowl of glaze as they are done.

5. Toss the crispy eggplant in the glaze, then transfer to a sheet pan. Roast until the glaze bakes onto the eggplant, being careful it doesn't burn, 5 to 7 minutes.

(RECIPE CONTINUES)

6. Meanwhile, fold the kimchi into the vegan mayo in a small bowl.

7. Warm the tortillas in the oven, directly on the rack, for about 2 minutes.

8. Assemble the tacos by spreading about 1 tablespoon of the kimchi mayo down the center of each tortilla. Top with a large spoonful of the roasted eggplant, dress with the cilantro and scallions, then serve.

tip: Our recent trip to Hong Kong exposed us to a melting pot of Asian cuisines from Japanese to Vietnamese. This menu offers some of the greatest hits of the Pacific Rim. Start off with a Kyoto Sour (page 225) served with Baby Cucumbers with *Sambal* and Peanuts (page 31) and Daikon "Summer Rolls" (page 32). Your guests can enjoy these eggplant tacos while you step away to plate the Soba Bowl with Shiitake *Dashi* and Market Greens (page 71).

desserts and baked goods

PEOPLE EAT DESSERT not because they're still hungry, but because it's delicious! From birthday cakes to warm cookies right out of the oven to a favorite pastry at a local bakery, desserts are comfort foods. You can try to cram a little nutrition into them, but at the end of the day, we seek them out simply to celebrate and indulge ourselves. They're good for the soul. At Vedge, we want our guests to save room for some of that indulgence, but we're also trying to push the experience further, offering inspired flavor combinations and techniques that put fruits and even some vegetables front and center.

apple cake fritters with waldorf frosting

PREP TIME: 20 MINUTES

COOK TIME: 20 MINUTES

MAKES 12 FRITTERS

1 tablespoon olive oil

1 large apple, such as Honey Crisp, peeled, cored, and chopped into ¼-inch dice

1 tablespoon light brown sugar

3 teaspoons ground cinnamon

3 cups all-purpose flour

2 teaspoons baking powder

2 teaspoons salt

4 teaspoons Ener-G egg replacer

1 cup vegan cream

Safflower oil

FROSTING

½ cup unsalted walnuts, toasted

8 ounces vegan cream cheese

¼ cup powdered sugar

½ teaspoon pure vanilla extract

½ teaspoon salt

¼ stalk celery, sliced into ⅛-inch dice

¼ cup raisins

Apples are one of the few fresh fruits you can get all fall and winter long, and once you get past the holiday season, this cinnamon-spiked apple dessert is the perfect homemade treat. At the restaurant, we serve these fritters fresh out of the fryer, topped with a frosting inspired by a classic Waldorf salad of apples, celery, and walnuts, all brought together with cream cheese-inspired icing. We have given you the frying instructions for when you're feeling extra indulgent, and there are baking directions for apple cupcakes as well.

1. Heat the olive oil in a large sauté pan over medium heat. Just before the oil starts to ripple, add the diced apple. Cook the apple, stirring occasionally, until it becomes tender, about 3 minutes. Stir in the brown sugar and continue cooking until it dissolves. Stir in 1 teaspoon of the cinnamon, remove the pan from the heat, and set aside to cool.

2. To make cupcakes, preheat the oven to 350°F and line a muffin pan with 12 liners.

3. Sift the flour into a medium bowl with the remaining 2 teaspoons cinnamon, the baking powder, and salt.

4. Whisk the Ener-G egg replacer powder with ⅓ cup water in a small bowl until it is smooth and fluffy, about 2 minutes. Stir in the vegan cream. Add to the flour mixture and stir until incorporated. Fold in the apples.

5. For fritters, heat a ¼-inch layer of safflower oil (or another oil with a high smoke point) in a medium saucepan over high heat. Once the oil begins to sizzle, fry four fritters at a time until golden brown on each side, about 4 minutes total. Lift from the oil and allow to drain on a paper towel and cool for a few minutes before frosting.

(RECIPE CONTINUES)

6. For cupcakes, fill each cupcake liner with about ¼ cup batter, or about two-thirds full. Bake until a toothpick inserted into the center of a cupcake comes out clean, 15 to 18 minutes. Remove from the oven and allow to cool fully before frosting.

7. Prepare the frosting by pulsing the walnuts in a food processor until they are broken into small pieces. Add the vegan cream cheese, powdered sugar, vanilla, and remaining ½ teaspoon salt and continue pulsing until combined and creamy. Transfer to a small bowl and fold in the celery and raisins.

8. Frost the cooled fritters or cupcakes and serve.

bbq cherries with jalapeño cornbread

PREP TIME: 20 MINUTES
BAKE TIME: 30 MINUTES
SERVES 12

CHERRIES

2 tablespoons olive oil

2 tablespoons agave nectar

½ teaspoon salt

¼ teaspoon ground allspice

¼ teaspoon ground cloves

1 pound whole cherries with stems (about 4 cups)

In the heat of the summer, eating cherries right off their stems and pits reminds me of eating corn on the cob—it's a fun, messy summer BBQ thing. Taking the extra step to grill the cherries gives them some savory flavor while maintaining their juicy punch. The cornbread also walks the sweet-savory line with the addition of jalapeño. It's spectacular on its own, but it makes an especially wonderful platform for these cherries— perhaps topped with a scoop of your favorite vegan ice cream.

1. To prepare the cherries, whisk together the olive oil, agave nectar, salt, allspice, and cloves in a large bowl. Toss the cherries in the mixture and set aside.

2. Preheat the oven to 350°F. Line a 13 x 9 x 2-inch baking pan with parchment paper.

3. To make the cornbread, sift the corn flour, all-purpose flour, cornmeal, baking powder, baking soda, and salt into a large bowl.

4. Combine the coconut milk, sugar, vegan butter, vegan shortening, barbecue sauce, and lime juice in a blender and blend until smooth.

5. Add the contents of the blender to the dry ingredients and stir just until incorporated. Fold in the jalapeño, then shave the ear of corn over the bowl to add the kernels to the batter. Stir again, just until incorporated.

6. Pour the batter into the prepared baking pan and bake until a toothpick inserted into the center comes out clean, 25 to 30 minutes. Cut into 12 slices, for serving. You will probably have some left over.

(INGREDIENTS CONTINUE)

(RECIPE CONTINUES)

7. Meanwhile, heat a grill pan or large sauté pan over high heat. (An outdoor grill is even better.) Sear the marinated cherries, about 1 cup at a time, just until the skin starts to blister, 2 to 3 minutes. Any remaining marinade can be used to make a syrup to drizzle over the cornbread. Simply reduce in a small saucepan over medium heat. Spoon the cherries over the cornbread and serve immediately.

tip: Ever since my first trip to Texas, I've always enjoyed a little kick in my cornbread. The addition of some zesty BBQ sauce and some jalapeño pepper complement the sweetness of the corn perfectly and can add some intrigue to your final dish. These accents can, of course, be omitted if you prefer something a little more tame. The Lemonade Ice Cream (page 180) also makes a fabulous addition to this dessert. And remember to remind your guests to watch out for the pits!

CORNBREAD

1½ cups corn flour

1 cup all-purpose flour

½ cup coarse cornmeal

1 teaspoon baking powder

1 teaspoon baking soda

1 teaspoon salt

One 13½-ounce can coconut milk

½ cup sugar

¼ cup vegan butter

¼ cup vegan shortening

2 tablespoons barbecue sauce

1 tablespoon freshly squeezed lime juice

¼ cup seeded, diced jalapeños

1 ear corn

beetroot *pots de crème*

PREP TIME: 10 MINUTES

COOK TIME: 5 MINUTES

SERVES 4 TO 6

2 cups bittersweet chocolate chips

1 cup coconut milk

1 teaspoon cornstarch

½ teaspoon salt

½ cup red beet juice

Every Valentine's Day, pastry chefs try to create new desserts that combine chocolate with something red or pink. Red velvet cake inevitably finds its way into the repertoire, and in the true Vedge spirit, I used the beet juice from my red velvet cake one year to infuse some chocolate truffles. It was a lovely combination, adding an extra dimension of earthiness to the bittersweet chocolate. These pots de crème showcase the same flavors in an intensely rich and decadent chocolate dessert. Just squeeze the gratings from about ½ a beet through a sieve to get the beet juice needed for this recipe. It's a good idea to wear plastic gloves so you don't stain your hands.

1. Place the chocolate chips in a medium bowl.

2. Heat the coconut milk in a small saucepan over medium heat. Stir in the cornstarch and salt, whisking to ensure that the cornstarch dissolves fully. The cornstarch will start to thicken the coconut milk after about 2 minutes. As soon as this happens, stir the beet juice into the warm coconut milk, then strain it through a sieve over the chocolate chips.

3. Whisk the chocolate mixture thoroughly until all of the chips are melted. Portion the mixture into serving dishes and chill for at least 1 hour to set. They will keep in the refrigerator, covered, for up to 4 days. The pots de crème are beautifully creamy at room temperature. Allow to sit for about one-half hour before serving.

tip: The chocolate swallows up the lovely color of the red beets, so just prior to serving, dust the *pots de crème* with a little bright pink beet powder (available at most spice shops).

blueberries with pie crust and lemonade ice cream

PREP TIME: 25 MINUTES,
PLUS EXTRA TIME FOR THE
ICE CREAM
COOK TIME: 45 MINUTES
SERVES: 6

ICE CREAM

1½ cups sugar

4 lemons

One 13½-ounce can coconut milk

1 cup vegan cream

½ teaspoon pure vanilla extract

PIE CRUST

1 cup all-purpose flour, plus more
for dusting

2 tablespoons sugar

½ teaspoon salt

1 tablespoon vegan butter, cold

1 tablespoon vegan shortening, cold

1 tablespoon olive oil

BLUEBERRIES

1 cup sugar

2 pints blueberries

2 tablespoons cornstarch

Pie is one of the best comfort foods of summertime. Served warm and topped with ice cream, it can't be beat. But nine times out of ten, it looks terrible after you slice it. On our dessert list at Vedge, we've offered deconstructed versions of pie that allow for more interesting and pretty plating. Here we've created a pie filling that can be heated to order, then topped with wedges of pie crust that act as a little shield to keep the lemonade ice cream from melting too soon. It's all the great flavors and textures of pie with a more elegant presentation. If you don't have an ice cream maker (or an extra 45 minutes), simply top with your favorite purchased vegan ice cream.

1. Begin by making the ice cream. Warm the sugar and 2 cups water in a medium saucepan over medium heat until the mixture reduces by half and thickens, about 12 minutes. Remove from the heat and allow to cool.

2. Zest two of the lemons, then juice all four lemons.

3. Transfer the contents of the saucepan to a blender. Add the coconut milk, vegan cream, vanilla extract, and lemon zest and juice and blend. Chill for about 30 minutes before transferring to an ice cream maker. Freeze the chilled base in the ice cream maker according to the manufacturer's instructions and then transfer to your freezer for at least 1 hour before serving. Store in the freezer up to 1 week.

4. To make the crust, combine the flour, sugar, and salt in a large bowl. Using a pastry cutter or metal fork, cut in the cold vegan butter and cold vegan shortening. Add the olive oil and continue cutting, until the mixture is sandy in consistency. Add ¼ to ⅓ cup cold water, a little at a time, just enough to hold the dough together. Form the dough into a soft ball, wrap it in plastic wrap and refrigerate for 10 minutes or until ready to use, up to 2 days.

(RECIPE CONTINUES)

5. Preheat the oven to 350°F and line a sheet pan with parchment paper. On a work surface dusted with flour, roll out the dough to about ¼ inch thick. Cut the dough into triangles or other shapes, then transfer to the parchment-lined sheet pan and bake until the pie crust pieces are golden brown, 6 to 8 minutes. Remove from the oven and cool fully, then store the pieces in an airtight container until ready to use.

6. In a medium saucepan, warm the sugar and 2 cups water over medium heat until the water boils, about 3 minutes, stirring to dissolve the sugar.

7. Carefully drop the blueberries into the boiling sugar water and blanch just until they plump up and the skins get tight and dark purple, about 1 minute. Transfer them with a slotted spoon to a bowl and allow them to cool at room temperature. Let the syrup continue to boil until it reduces by three-quarters, 5 to 7 minutes.

8. In a small bowl, create a slurry by combining 2 tablespoons of the hot syrup and the cornstarch and stirring until the cornstarch is dissolved. Add the slurry to the remaining syrup in the saucepan. Stir to combine, then remove from the heat.

9. Allow the thickened syrup to cool, about 10 minutes, then fold in the blanched blueberries.

10. Transfer the blueberries to serving dishes, and garnish with the wedges of pie crust and a scoop of the ice cream. Serve immediately.

caramel *panna cotta* with red raspberries and tarragon

PREP TIME: 10 MINUTES,
PLUS 2 HOURS CHILLING TIME
COOK TIME: 30 MINUTES
SERVES 8

¼ cup sugar

Two 13½-ounce cans coconut milk

Seeds from ¼ vanilla bean pod

1 teaspoon pure vanilla extract

½ teaspoon agar

½ teaspoon salt

2 teaspoons tarragon leaves, chopped

1 teaspoon agave nectar

1 teaspoon freshly squeezed lemon juice

1 pint raspberries

Panna cotta, or cooked cream, is a traditional dessert from the Piedmont region of Italy. At Vedge we use agar in place of gelatin to help set this custard. And we create a caramel flavor by cooking the sugar first for the base layer of our custard. The rich creamy custard is an ideal canvas for serving any fresh fruit. In this case, the equal parts lemon and agave create a light syrup to help the berries shine, and the tarragon adds a hint of fresh herbal interest.

1. Heat the sugar in a large saucepan over medium heat until it starts to caramelize, stirring occasionally to prevent burning, about 5 minutes.

2. Once the sugar has turned amber but before it burns, slowly and carefully stir in the coconut milk. Add the vanilla bean seeds, vanilla extract, agar, and salt. Bring back to a simmer, then stir occasionally until the agar has dissolved thoroughly, 8 to 10 minutes.

3. Transfer the mixture to the blender and puree for 1 minute.

4. Portion the coconut milk mixture into eight 4-ounce ramekins. Cool at room temperature for about 20 minutes before transferring to the refrigerator. Chill for at least 2 hours.

5. Meanwhile, toss the chopped tarragon in a small bowl with the agave and lemon juice. Add the berries and toss gently, then cover the bowl and transfer it to the refrigerator until ready to serve, up to 1 day.

6. When ready to serve, run a small knife around the edge of each custard to help release it from the ramekin. Invert it onto a serving dish, using the knife to guide it out. Arrange some dressed berries on top or on the side and serve.

chocolate stuffed beignets

PREP TIME: 20 MINUTES,
PLUS 1 HOUR RISING TIME
COOK TIME: 30 MINUTES
MAKES 24 BEIGNETS

1/4 cup granulated sugar

1 1/2 teaspoons active dry yeast

3 1/2 cups all-purpose flour

1 teaspoon baking powder

1/2 teaspoon salt

1/2 cup vegan cream

2 tablespoons vegan shortening

1 cup bittersweet chocolate chips

1 cup powdered sugar

1 teaspoon ground cinnamon (optional)

4 cups canola oil for frying

This recipe was created long before my first trip to New Orleans. I wanted something on our menu that was sinfully delicious and addictive—the kind of thing you feel guilty for eating. In the winter months, I serve these beignets with a mug of seriously decadent hot chocolate; in the summer, I pair them with an iced coffee float. They are easy to make, can be prepared in advance, and give very indulgent results. I think the folks at Café du Monde in NOLA would approve!

1. Stir together the granulated sugar and yeast in a small bowl with 1 cup warm water (about 110°F). Once the sugar is fully dissolved, set the mixture aside for about 20 minutes to let the yeast activate.

2. Meanwhile, sift the flour, baking powder, and salt into a large bowl.

3. Warm the vegan cream and vegan shortening in a small saucepan over low heat just until the shortening dissolves, about 5 minutes. Stir the cream mixture and add it to the flour mixture. Stir until just combined.

4. Add the yeast mixture and begin kneading with your hands until the dough is smooth, about 2 minutes.

5. Cover the dough with a kitchen towel or plastic wrap and set aside in a warm area to rise for 1 hour.

6. Line a sheet pan with parchment paper. Cut the dough into four sections, then cut each section into six chunks. Flatten each chunk into a little disk and place about 10 chocolate chips in the center. Bring all the edges up to meet each other like a little Chinese dumpling, then pinch together a tight seam. Set the sealed beignets on the prepared sheet pan. You can refrigerate the stuffed beignets or keep them at room temperature for up to 30 minutes while you heat your fryer.

(RECIPE CONTINUES)

7. Meanwhile, sift the powdered sugar and cinnamon (if using) into a medium bowl and set aside. Heat the canola oil in a medium saucepan to 365°F, using a deep-fry- or candy thermometer to measure the temperature. (A countertop fryer will also work beautifully, if you have one.)

8. Heat the canola oil in a medium saucepan to 365°F, using a deep-fry- or candy thermometer to measure the temperature. (A countertop fryer will also work beautifully, if you have one.) Fry four beignets at a time for 4 minutes each, flipping them halfway through cooking. Remove the beignets with a slotted spoon and transfer to a plate lined with paper towels. Let the beignets rest for 20 seconds before lightly tossing them in the bowl of powdered sugar. Serve immediately.

figgy toffee pudding with madeira-quince ice cream

PREP TIME: 10 MINUTES,
PLUS EXTRA TIME FOR THE
ICE CREAM
COOK TIME: 1½ HOURS
SERVES 12

As soon as the leaves start to fall, some version of sticky toffee pudding goes on the dessert menu at Vedge. And we leave it there, happily, until spring. Immensely popular in British culture, this salty-sweet treat ranks among the top comfort food desserts. We served this version at *Cooking Light* magazine's 2012 "Light Up the Night" event in New York. It was late September, and the crowd was chomping at the bit for a transition into fall, so this dessert was enthusiastically welcomed. Figs add depth to the sweet toffee sauce, and the rich, nutty sweetness of Madeira combines with the floral honey notes of quince for a unique ice cream, perfect to top the cake or enjoy on its own. If quinces are unavailable, Williams or Bartlett pears make a nice stand-in. And if you don't have an ice cream maker (or an extra 45 minutes), simply top the puddings with your favorite purchased vegan ice cream.

ICE CREAM

1 cup granulated sugar

½ cup Madeira (see Tip), preferably Blandy's 5-Year-Old Alvada

2 quince, cored and diced

1 cup vegan cream

1 teaspoon freshly squeezed lemon juice

1 teaspoon pure vanilla extract

CAKE

3 cups all-purpose flour

2 teaspoons ground cinnamon

1 teaspoon baking powder

½ teaspoon salt

1 cup pitted, dried dates

1 cup packed light brown sugar

1 cup granulated sugar

¼ cup vegan butter

¼ cup vegan shortening

1. Begin by making the ice cream. Bring the sugar, Madeira, and 1½ cups water to a boil in a medium saucepan over high heat. Add the diced quinces and cook until very soft, about 12 minutes.

2. Transfer the mixture to a blender, and add the vegan cream, lemon juice, and vanilla. Blend until smooth, strain through a sieve, and chill for 30 minutes before transferring to an ice cream maker.

3. Freeze the chilled base in the ice cream maker according to the manufacturer's instructions and then transfer to your freezer for at least 1 hour before serving. Store in the freezer until ready to use, up to 1 week.

4. Next make the cake. Preheat the oven to 350°F. Line a 13 x 9 x 2-inch pan with parchment paper.

5. Combine the flour, cinnamon, baking powder, and salt in a large bowl.

(RECIPE CONTINUES)

(INGREDIENTS CONTINUE)

FIGGY TOFFEE SAUCE

2 cups packed light brown sugar

1 cup vegan cream

¼ cup vegan butter

1 teaspoon pure vanilla extract

½ teaspoon salt

1 pint fresh Black Mission figs, stems removed, quartered

6. Combine the dried dates, brown and granulated sugars, vegan butter, vegan shortening, and 2 cups water in a blender and blend until evenly mixed. A few chunks of date is OK. Make sure there are no pits.

7. Add the contents of the blender to the dry ingredients, and stir just until combined. Pour the batter into the prepared pan. Bake for 15 minutes, rotate the pan, and continue baking until a toothpick inserted into the center comes out clean, an additional 15 to 20 minutes.

8. Meanwhile, make the figgy toffee sauce. Combine the brown sugar, vegan cream, vegan butter, vanilla, and salt in a medium saucepan. Heat over medium heat, stirring occasionally, until the sugar dissolves, about 10 minutes. Add the figs and continue cooking until the sugars start to caramelize and the figs start to melt, about 5 minutes longer.

9. Assemble the dessert by placing a slice of the warm cake in a bowl. Top the cake with about 3 tablespoons of the figgy toffee sauce. Place a scoop of the ice cream on top and serve immediately.

tip: Madeira is a wonderful wine to keep behind your bar. It is gorgeous to sip on its own, and it can add beautiful, nutty, and sweet tones to both savory and sweet cooking. Because it's already heated to achieve its characteristic concentration of flavor, it's virtually impossible to denature it any further. So go ahead and invest in a nice little bottle; use it in your cooking and baking, and definitely remember to enjoy a glass with your figgy toffee pudding!

cranberry jelly doughnuts with hot cider

PREP TIME: 20 MINUTES
COOK TIME: 75 MINUTES
SERVES 8

DOUGH

¼ cup sugar

2 teaspoons active dry yeast

3½ cups all-purpose flour

½ teaspoon baking powder

½ teaspoon salt

½ cup vegan cream

2 tablespoons vegan shortening

JELLY

1 cup fresh cranberries

½ cup sugar

There are plenty of fun things to do with fresh cranberries beyond making sauce for Thanksgiving. With the natural burst of tart flavor, they make a delicious filling for a traditional jelly doughnut. The dough can be made ahead of time—in fact, the flavor of the dough will improve over a day or two as the yeast develops—and you can fry up just a few doughnuts at a time. The pear-infused cider is an ideal accompaniment for the doughnuts or can be enjoyed on its own, perhaps served piping hot with a splash of dark rum.

1. Begin by making the dough. Whisk together ¾ cup warm water (about 110°F), the sugar, and the yeast in a small bowl. Set aside for at least 15 minutes.

2. Meanwhile, sift the flour, baking powder, and salt into a medium bowl.

3. Heat the vegan cream and vegan shortening in a small saucepan over low heat just until the shortening has melted, about 5 minutes. Remove from the heat and allow to cool to room temperature.

4. Add the yeast mixture and the cooled cream mixture to the flour mixture. Stir, then knead until you form a smooth dough ball, about 5 minutes. If using right away, cover the dough with a kitchen towel and set aside in a warm place for at least 45 minutes. Alternatively, you can wrap the dough ball in plastic wrap and refrigerate until ready to use, up to 24 hours.

5. Meanwhile, make the jelly by combining 1 cup water with the cranberries and sugar in a medium saucepan. Heat over medium heat until the cranberries burst and become very soft, 10 to 12 minutes. Remove the cranberries with a slotted spoon, transfer them to a blender, and blend until smooth. Return the cranberry puree to the

(INGREDIENTS CONTINUE)

(RECIPE CONTINUES)

cooking syrup and continue to cook until it thickens and is reduced by half, about 10 minutes.

6. Next, combine all of the cider ingredients in a medium saucepan. Heat over medium heat until the pears are very soft, 10 minutes. Carefully strain the cider into a bowl. Discard the pears, cinnamon stick, and star anise.

7. Heat the canola oil in a medium saucepan to 365°F, using a deep-fry- or candy thermometer to measure the temperature. (A countertop fryer will also work beautifully, if you have one.)

8. Cut the dough into sixteen pieces. Carefully fry four pieces of dough at a time until golden brown on both sides, 3 to 4 minutes, flipping occasionally. Transfer to a plate lined with paper towels to rest before dusting in extra sugar.

9. Fill a pastry injector with the jelly and squirt about 1 tablespoon into the center of each doughnut. You can also use a toothpick to poke a hole in the back of the doughnut, create a makeshift pastry bag with a resealable plastic bag, fill it with the jelly, and squeeze. Serve the doughnuts with a small cup of the warm cider.

tip: To fill these doughnuts like a professional you'll need a pastry injector (like a giant syringe); they're available at most cooking and baking supply stores and online.

CIDER

4 cups apple cider

2 pears, cored and chopped

1 cinnamon stick

1 small star anise

1 teaspoon blackstrap molasses

Dash of ground allspice

Dash of ground cloves

4 cups canola oil for frying

1 cup sugar for dusting

summer corn custard with blackberries and hazelnuts

PREP TIME: 25 MINUTES,
PLUS 2 HOURS CHILLING TIME
COOK TIME: 20 MINUTES
SERVES 6

2 ears corn

1½ cups vegan cream

1 cup coconut milk

3 tablespoons agave nectar

1 teaspoon pure vanilla extract

1 teaspoon salt

½ teaspoon agar

1 tablespoon cornstarch

2 cups blackberries, halved

2 sage leaves, cut into chiffonade

1 teaspoon freshly squeezed lemon juice

½ cup shelled, skinned hazelnuts, chopped

Incorporating vegetables into desserts can be tricky, but corn is what we call "a gimme." This recipe captures the sweetness of summer corn and presents it with a fun, creamy texture. Here we use agar, a gelatin substitute made from seaweed to set our custard. It's perfectly balanced with the juicy, tart pop of blackberries and a toasty crunch of hazelnuts—a simple recipe that yields elegant results.

1. Shave the corn kernels off the cobs into a medium saucepan.

2. Add the vegan cream, coconut milk, 2 tablespoons of the agave, the vanilla, ½ teaspoon of the salt, and the agar. Heat over medium heat, stirring occasionally, until it comes to a boil, about 10 minutes. Keep the mixture at a rolling boil for about 5 minutes to allow the agar to fully dissolve, stirring occasionally.

3. Carefully transfer the mixture to a blender. Add the cornstarch and blend for 30 seconds.

4. Strain the contents through a sieve into a clean saucepan, bring just to a boil, and immediately remove from the heat. Ladle the custard into six heat-resistant ramekins or serving dishes.

5. Allow the custards to cool at room temperature for 30 minutes before transferring to the refrigerator. Let them chill for at least 2 hours before serving.

6. Toss the blackberries in a small bowl with the sage, lemon juice, and remaining 1 tablespoon agave. Cover and refrigerate until ready to use.

7. Place the hazelnuts in a small sauté pan, sprinkle with the remaining ½ teaspoon salt, and dry-toast over medium-low heat until the nuts are nicely golden brown, about 6 minutes. Allow the nuts to cool, then store them in an airtight container.

8. When the custards are ready to serve, toss the hazelnuts with the blackberries, then spoon some on top of each custard. Serve immediately.

There is such a short window each summer when peaches are truly exceptional. The best peaches smell heavenly at room temperature and just start to give a little under pressure from your fingers. Here we peel the peaches for texture, but we take advantage of the gorgeous flavor from the peach skins in our ice cream syrup. Toasted pecans make for a rich ice cream that is a wonderful complement to perfectly ripe, slightly tart peaches, but if you don't have an ice cream maker—or an extra 45 minutes—substitute your favorite purchased vegan ice cream.

PREP TIME: 10 MINUTES,
PLUS EXTRA TIME FOR THE
ICE CREAM
COOK TIME: 30 MINUTES
SERVES 5

PEACHES

3 peaches

1 cup bourbon, preferably Bulleit

½ cup granulated sugar

½ vanilla bean pod, split, or
2 teaspoons pure vanilla extract

ICE CREAM

1½ cups unsalted pecan pieces

½ cup brown sugar

¼ cup all-purpose flour

3 tablespoons vegan butter

1 teaspoon salt

2 cups vegan cream

1. Peel the peaches, reserving the skin. Slice the peaches in half, remove the pits, and slice each half into three or four wedges no less than ½ inch thick.

2. Bring 5 cups water to a boil in a medium saucepan over high heat. Add the bourbon, sugar, and vanilla bean pod. Reduce the heat to medium-high.

3. In small batches (about 1 cup of peach wedges at a time), lightly poach the peaches just until they start to soften, about 1 minute. Use a slotted spoon to transfer the peaches to a bowl and allow them to cool at room temperature. The poached peaches can be stored in an airtight container in the refrigerator for up 3 days. They can be served chilled or at room temperature.

4. Add the peach skins to the boiling syrup and continue to cook over medium-high heat until the syrup has reduced by half, about 10 minutes. Strain the syrup through a sieve into a medium bowl and allow to cool.

(RECIPE CONTINUES)

5. Meanwhile, make the ice cream. Toast the pecans in a large sauté pan over medium heat, stirring occasionally, until they are golden brown, about 4 minutes. Remove the pan from the heat and add the brown sugar, flour, vegan butter, and salt. Return the pan to the heat and continue cooking for another 5 minutes or until the flour has turned golden brown. Remove from the heat and allow to cool. Set aside about ½ cup of this mixture for the garnish; it can be stored in an airtight container for up to 1 week.

6. Combine the peach syrup with the remaining toasted pecans in a blender with the vegan cream and blend until smooth. Some chunks of pecan will remain; you can strain them if you prefer a smooth ice cream.Chill for about 30 minutes before transferring to an ice cream maker.

7. Freeze the chilled base in the ice cream maker according to the manufacturer's instructions and then transfer to your freezer for at least 1 hour before serving. Store in the freezer until ready to use, up to 1 week.

8. To assemble the dessert, arrange five peach wedges in individual dishes or bowls and place a scoop of ice cream directly on top. Drizzle with the syrup they created while cooling and sprinkle with the toasted pecan garnish.

tip: You can use leftover vanilla bean pods to make vanilla-infused olive oil and sugar. For the oil, add 1 spent vanilla bean pod to ½ cup olive oil and store in an airtight container in a cool dark place for at least 48 hours and up to 2 weeks. For the sugar, add 1 spent vanilla bean pod to 1 cup of sugar in an airtight container and store in a cool dark place over-night and for up to 2 weeks.

strawberry sorrel bread pudding with saffron ice cream

PREP TIME: 30 MINUTES, PLUS EXTRA TIME FOR THE ICE CREAM

COOK TIME: 1½ HOURS

SERVES 12

I created this dessert for a James Beard House dinner back in 2010, and I always run a version of it when strawberries are in season. There is something magical about the candy sweetness of lightly baked strawberries, and here the rhubarb and sorrel (or, if you can't find it, basil) challenge this sweetness with bright, sour-tart flavors. The saffron ice cream provides a creamy note to bring it all together. (Although if you don't have an ice cream maker—or an extra 45 minutes—substitute your favorite purchased vegan ice cream. This dish is as visually appealing as it is delicious, and while it's labor intensive, all of the components can be prepared ahead of time.

1. First, make the cake. Preheat the oven to 375°F. Line a 13 x 9 x 2-inch baking pan with parchment paper.

2. Sift the flour, baking powder, baking soda, and salt into a large bowl.

3. Combine the remaining ingredients in a blender and blend until smooth. Pour the contents of the blender into the bowl of dry ingredients and whisk until just mixed.

4. Pour the batter into the prepared baking pan and bake for 25 minutes. Rotate the pan, then continue baking until a toothpick inserted into the center of the cake comes out clean, about 10 more minutes.

5. Allow the cake to cool for at least 1 hour. If preparing the dessert immediately, cut the cake into ½-inch cubes. Otherwise, store the cake in the refrigerator, covered, for up to 5 days.

6. While the cake is baking, make the sorrel sauce. Whisk together the vegan cream, agave, and flour in a small bowl. Set aside.

CAKE

3 cups all-purpose flour

1½ teaspoons baking powder

½ teaspoon baking soda

½ teaspoon salt

2 cups sugar

1½ cups coconut milk

¾ cup vegan butter

½ cup vegan cream

¼ cup vegan shortening

Zest of ½ lemon

(RECIPE CONTINUES)   (INGREDIENTS CONTINUE)

SORREL SAUCE

¼ cup vegan cream

2 tablespoons agave nectar

2 tablespoons all-purpose flour

1 cup firmly packed fresh sorrel

½ teaspoon pure vanilla extract

¼ teaspoon salt

2 tablespoons olive oil

RHUBARB NECTAR

3 stalks rhubarb, roughly chopped

½ cup sugar

ICE CREAM

2 cups sugar

1 teaspoon saffron

2¼ cups coconut milk

2¼ cups vegan cream

¾ teaspoon salt

1 pint strawberries, hulled, chopped

7. Pulse the sorrel, vanilla, and salt in a food processor until the sorrel leaves are coarsely chopped. Add the olive oil, then pulse again. Add the cream mixture and pulse again to combine evenly. Store the sorrel sauce in an airtight container in the refrigerator for up to 2 days.

8. Next, make the rhubarb nectar by combining the rhubarb, sugar, and 1 cup water in a medium saucepan. Simmer over medium heat until the rhubarb is soft, about 5 minutes.

9. Carefully transfer the mixture to a blender and blend until smooth.

10. Allow the mixture to cool fully, then store in an airtight container in the refrigerator for up to 1 week.

11. Finally, make the saffron ice cream. Combine 2 cups water and the sugar in a medium saucepan over medium heat, stirring occasionally. Bring to a slow boil and allow to reduce by one-quarter, about 5 minutes, to make a syrup. Remove the pan from the heat, add the saffron, and set aside to cool for about 20 minutes.

12. Transfer the cooled syrup to a blender and add the coconut milk, vegan cream, and salt. Chill for about 30 minutes.

13. Freeze the chilled base in the ice cream maker according to the manufacturer's instructions and then transfer to your freezer for at least 1 hour before serving. Store in the freezer until ready to use, up to 1 week.

14. When ready to assemble the dessert, preheat the oven to 350°F.

15. Toss about 6 cups of the cake cubes in a medium bowl with the chopped strawberries and about 1 cup of the sorrel sauce. Transfer the mixture to a 13 x 9 x 2-inch baking pan and warm in the oven for about 10 minutes.

16. Scoop ½-cup portions of the warmed bread pudding into serving dishes. Streak the dishes with rhubarb nectar, top the pudding with a scoop of the saffron ice cream, and serve immediately.

I get no greater satisfaction than knowing we've snuck some sweet potatoes and red cabbage onto the dessert menu at Vedge. This dish was originally inspired by a trip to the Czech Republic, where I enjoyed plum dumplings dusted in powdered sugar and served with vegan sour cream. Here, we fill our turnovers with candied whipped sweet potato, and the kraut garnish offers a nice bright note from the sweet Riesling. If you want to go all out, try serving them with a dollop of vegan sour cream whipped with a little powdered sugar and orange zest.

1. To make the sweet potato filling, bring a medium pot of salted water to a boil over high heat. Boil the sweet potato chunks just until tender, about 10 minutes.

2. Drain the potatoes, reserving ¼ cup of the cooking water.

3. Transfer the hot potatoes and reserved cooking water, the brown sugar, vegan butter, vanilla, and salt to a medium bowl. Beat with a hand mixer until totally smooth, then set aside to fully cool.

4. Meanwhile, make the sweet kraut. Heat the oil in a medium sauté pan over medium heat. Add the cabbage and allow it to start to sear for about 3 minutes, then add the brown sugar and spices. Let the sugar start to melt with the cabbage juice for another 3 minutes, then add the Riesling. Allow the cabbage to cook down and steam itself for another 8 to 10 minutes. The cabbage will now be dark pink instead of purple. Remove the pan from the heat and let it cool fully.

sweet potato turnovers with sweet kraut

PREP TIME: 30 MINUTES

COOK TIME: 1 HOUR

SERVES 6

SWEET POTATO FILLING

1 large sweet potato, peeled and chopped into 1-inch chunks

½ cup packed light brown sugar

3 tablespoons vegan butter

1½ teaspoons pure vanilla extract

½ teaspoon salt

SWEET KRAUT

1 tablespoon olive oil

2 cups thinly sliced red cabbage (approximately ¼ head, outer leaves and stem removed)

¼ cup packed light brown sugar

½ teaspoon ground cinnamon

Pinch of ground allspice

Pinch of ground cloves

1 cup sweet Riesling

(RECIPE CONTINUES)

(INGREDIENTS CONTINUE)

TURNOVER CRUST

1 cup all-purpose flour, plus more for dusting

1 tablespoon vegan butter, cold

1 tablespoon vegan shortening, cold

2 tablespoons granulated sugar

1 tablespoon olive oil

½ teaspoon ground cinnamon

½ teaspoon salt

¼ teaspoon ground allspice

5. While the potatoes and kraut are cooling, make the turnover crust. Pulse together the flour, vegan butter, and vegan shortening until it looks chunky and sandy. Add the sugar, olive oil, cinnamon, salt, and allspice and pulse again. While pulsing, slowly drizzle in 2 to 3 tablespoons cold water, little by little—just until a loose dough ball is formed and spins around the bowl of the food processor. Wrap the dough in plastic wrap and refrigerate for at least 10 minutes or up to 2 days.

6. Preheat the oven to 400°F. Line a sheet pan with parchment paper.

7. On a work surface dusted with flour, roll out the dough to ¼ inch thick. Use a 4-inch-wide circle cutter to stamp out the turnover shells. Place 1 heaping tablespoon of the sweet potato filling in the center of each dough circle. Bring the edges of the circle together, forming a half circle, and pinch them together tightly. Use a fork to crimp the edges of the seal. Arrange the turnovers on the prepared sheet pan.

8. Bake the turnovers until golden brown, 10 to 12 minutes. Remove from the oven and allow to cool slightly. Arrange on serving dishes with the sweet kraut and serve.

zucchini bread french toast

PREP TIME: 25 MINUTES

COOK TIME: 1½ HOURS

SERVES 8

Zucchini invariably turns into a gardener's August night-mare. If you have friends with green thumbs, they will almost certainly be eyeing you to see just how much they might be able to unload on you. Here are two separate recipes, each enjoyable on its own, that come together for an unusual late-summer dessert. The recipes double and triple easily, depending on just how much zucchini you're trying to move out.

ZUCCHINI BREAD

½ cup whole wheat flour

½ cup all-purpose flour

1 teaspoon ground cinnamon

¼ teaspoon ground nutmeg

1 teaspoon baking powder

1 teaspoon baking soda

½ teaspoon salt

1 cup light brown sugar

4 tablespoons vegan butter

⅓ cup olive oil

¾ cup vegan sour cream

⅓ cup vegan cream

2 teaspoons pure vanilla extract

1 teaspoon apple cider vinegar

2 cups finely grated zucchini (about ¼ pound)

1. First, make the zucchini bread. Preheat the oven to 350°F. Line a loaf pan with parchment paper.

2. Sift the all-purpose and whole wheat flours, cinnamon, baking powder, baking soda, nutmeg, and salt into a large bowl.

3. Combine the light brown sugar, vegan butter, olive oil, vegan sour cream, vegan cream, vanilla and vinegar in a blender. Blend until smooth.

4. Add the contents of the blender to the bowl of dry ingredients and stir just until combined. Stir in the grated zucchini.

5. Transfer the batter to the prepared pan and bake for 35 minutes. Rotate the pan, then continue baking until a toothpick inserted into the center comes out clean, about 30 more minutes. Allow the loaf to fully cool in the pan, about 1 hour. When cool, slice the zucchini bread into eight ¾-inch-thick slices.

(RECIPE CONTINUES)

(INGREDIENTS CONTINUE)

FRENCH TOAST BATTER

½ cup coconut milk

½ cup vegan cream

3 tablespoons all-purpose flour

1 tablespoon pure maple syrup

1 teaspoon baking powder

½ teaspoon ground cinnamon

¼ teaspoon ground allspice

¼ teaspoon ground cloves

Olive oil for searing the bread

Pure maple syrup, vegan butter, and fruit for garnish (optional)

6. Meanwhile, combine all of the French toast batter ingredients in a medium bowl and whisk until smooth. Transfer to a wide, shallow bowl.

7. Heat a large sauté pan over medium-high heat and add about 1 tablespoon of olive oil.

8. Dip the zucchini bread into the batter, one or two slices at a time, coating all sides evenly. Carefully place the slices in the sauté pan. Sear for 2 minutes, then flip and cook for an additional 1½ minutes. Transfer to a serving dish and tent lightly with foil, or to a 300°F oven. Repeat with the remaining slices of bread.

9. Serve immediately with maple syrup, vegan butter, or fresh fruit if desired.

breads

BAKING BREAD INVOLVES a surprising amount of variation because bread is highly responsive to its environment. One of the most crucial steps is proofing, a period of time when you are allowing the yeast to rise and create structure in the dough. Proofing in the Vedge kitchen is very different in the warm, humid months of July and August compared to the cold, dryer months of January and February.

Some of our recipes call for a poolish; this is a fermentation starter made of equal parts flour and water with a pinch of yeast that enhances the flavors and textures of certain breads. We keep our poolish or starter refrigerated overnight in warmer months, left out at room temperature in cooler months. Take this into account when storing poolish or starter and when proofing dough in your home kitchen. Proofing helps to create the right structure inside your bread, and the process of kneading and forming is what achieves a gorgeous crust.

We're measuring in grams here, but we provide standard measurements for those without kitchen scales. Using a scale to measure ingredients is best, but if you don't have a scale, you can still make tasty bread. With a little practice, even beginner bakers will find that these recipes make it possible to serve delicious, homemade bread alongside any dish in this book.

Fresh bread trumps store-bought any day. At Vedge, we make our house bread every single morning. For those few of us who have had the pleasure of coming in early in the morning and getting the kitchen all to ourselves, this is a magical time. And while this recipe is definitely involved, once you have tried it a few times, the results will be well worth your efforts. Rather than keep a starter in the fridge that has to be fed every day, we use a poolish to achieve just a little sourdough flavor by allowing the yeasts to develop overnight in advance of making the rest of the dough.

1. Make the poolish by combining 340 grams (1½ cups) cold water with the bread flour and yeast in a large food-safe, sealable bowl. Stir very well, leaving no clumps. Seal the bowl and let the mixture sit for 8 to 12 hours at room temperature during cooler months or in the refrigerator during warmer months. Be prepared for it to double in size, depending on the temperature.

2. When ready to make the dough, combine the bread flour with the salt and yeast in a stand mixer fitted with a dough hook and mix for 5 minutes, or mix by hand for about 12 minutes. Add the poolish from the bowl and 415 grams (1¾ cups) cold water. Mix until a stretchy dough ball is formed, about 5 minutes.

3. Dust a clean work surface and your hands with flour. Transfer the dough ball to the work surface. Viewing the dough ball like a clock, reach your fingertips under the 2:00 position and stretch it up and over to the 6:00 position. Use your palms to continue rolling the dough under itself and back to the starting position. Repeat this process about ten times, each time trying to develop a taut outer skin on the dough ball. Imagine that the dough ball is an inflated balloon and each time you make the fold, the surface tension increases. Transfer the ball to a bowl, cover with plastic wrap, and let it rest in a warm spot for 45 minutes.

house bread

PREP TIME: 2 HOURS,
PLUS 8 TO 12 HOURS FOR
POOLISH PREP
COOK TIME: 20 MINUTES
MAKES 1 LARGE LOAF

POOLISH

340 grams (2½ cups) bread flour

Pinch of active dry yeast

DOUGH

805 grams (6 cups) bread flour, plus more for dusting

15 grams (2 teaspoons) salt

7 grams (1½ teaspoon) active dry yeast

DESSERTS AND BAKED GOODS   207

4. Return the dough ball to the work surface and repeat the folding process, then return it to the bowl, cover with plastic wrap, and let it rest in a warm spot for another 30 minutes.

5. Line a sheet pan with parchment paper. Return the dough ball to the work surface. Again, viewing the ball as a clock, use your fingertips to fold the 3:00 position into the center, then fold the 9:00 position into the center. Next, fold the 12:00 position into the center. Locate the new 12:00 position on the reshaped dough ball and pull it up and to the bottom. Use your palms again to continue rolling the dough under itself and now out to the right and left sides, allowing the ball to form a rectangle. Little air bubbles may pop as air gets pushed from the center. Transfer the loaf to the prepared sheet pan. Cover loosely with plastic wrap and leave it in a warm place for 15 minutes.

6. Preheat the oven to 400°F. Pour about 2 cups water into a small pan and place it in the oven to generate moisture while the bread bakes.

7. Remove the plastic wrap from the loaf. Using a serrated knife, score the loaf four times diagonally across the top.

8. Bake for 8 minutes, rotate the pan halfway, remove the pan of water, then continue baking for an additional 5 minutes.

9. Turn off the oven, and leave the door slightly ajar. Let the loaf continue baking for 8 minutes.

10. Remove the bread from the oven and transfer to a wire rack to cool fully, 1 to 2 hours. Slice and serve.

nine-seed rye bread

PREP TIME: 2 HOURS

BAKE TIME: 30 MINUTES

MAKES 1 LOAF

If you're new to bread baking, this is a straightforward recipe that doesn't require much planning ahead. Be creative and use nine different seeds of your choice. Or stick with something simple and use a seed you know you like. Feel free to adjust the spices to your own preferences. This bread goes especially well with the Eastern European dishes in the book, such as Kohlrabi Salad with White Beans and Horse-radish (page 38) and Spiced Little Carrots with Chickpea-Sauerkraut Puree (page 49).

5 grams (2 teaspoons) sugar

7 grams (1½ teaspoons) active dry yeast

10 grams (1 tablespoon) total of your preferred seed mix such as white sesame, black sesame, fennel, celery, poppy, cumin, dill, caraway, and flax

15 grams (2 teaspoons) salt

650 grams (5½ cups) bread flour, plus more for dusting

200 grams (1¾ cups) rye flour

15 grams (1 tablespoon) blackstrap molasses

15 grams (1 tablespoon) olive oil

1. Stir the sugar and yeast into 500 grams (2¼ cups) cold water in a small bowl.

2. Grind the seeds separately in a coffee mill until you achieve a small uniform size.

3. Mix together the salt and spice mix with the bread and rye flours in a large bowl until the spices are evenly distributed.

4. Stir the molasses and olive oil into the yeast mixture. Add this liquid mixture to the flour mixture and begin kneading until the dough comes together in a ball. The dough should be soft but should not stick to your fingers too much.

5. Turn the dough ball out on a flour-dusted work surface, then use your fingers to pull the top right corner down to the bottom. Create a new seal by pressing your palms into the bottom of the ball. Repeat this fold six times to create a smooth surface. Place the dough ball back in the kneading bowl, cover with plastic wrap, and set aside in a warm area to proof for 1 hour.

6. Preheat the oven to 400°F. Line a sheet pan with parchment paper.

(RECIPE CONTINUES)

7. Transfer the dough ball back to the work surface and form into a loaf shape. Try folding like an envelope, with the right side of the dough ball into the center, the left side into the center, the top to the center, then the new top to the very bottom, each time stretching the exterior surface of the dough. Use your palms to create a seal at the bottom, rolling from the center to the two ends. You should have a slightly oval shape. Lift this onto the prepared sheet pan. Cover loosely with plastic wrap, then set aside in a warm area to proof for an additional 30 minutes.

8. Score the bread with a serrated knife three times across the top. Bake for 10 minutes, rotate the pan, then continue baking for an additional 10 minutes. Open the oven door, turn off the oven, and leave the bread inside with the door ajar for 10 minutes to start a gradual cooling process. Remove the pan from the oven and allow the bread to fully cool on a wire rack for at least 1 hour before slicing.

pumpernickel bread

PREP TIME: 1½ HOURS

COOK TIME: 1 HOUR

MAKES 1 LOAF

An authentic pumpernickel bread is a worthy addition to any home baking repertoire. It should have a nice crust while remaining moist inside, and a rich flavor with dark, chocolaty bitter tones. Use this bread to make hearty sandwiches.

1. Combine 280 grams (1¼ cups) warm water (about 110°F) with the yeast and sugar. Stir, then set aside at room temperature for at least 15 minutes.

2. Meanwhile, sift the all-purpose flour, rye flour, bran, whole-wheat flour, and salt into a large bowl. Add the caraway seeds.

3. In a medium saucepan, combine 220 grams (1 cup) water with the chocolate, vegan butter, molasses, apple cider vinegar, and coffee granules. Heat over low heat, stirring occasionally, just until the chocolate and vegan butter melt. Remove from the heat and cool at room temperature for 10 to 15 minutes, stirring occasionally so that it doesn't solidify.

4. Add the yeast mixture to the chocolate mixture in the pan, stir, then add that to the flour mixture in the bowl. Knead with your hands for about 5 minutes to form a dough.

5. Line a sheet pan with parchment paper. Transfer the dough to a work surface dusted with flour and work the dough into a ball. If the dough is sticky, try adding a tablespoon or two of flour to make it easier to handle.

6. Shape into a loaf, then set on the prepared sheet pan. Cover the loaf loosely with plastic wrap and set aside in a warm place for 1 hour. The dough should nearly double in size.

7. Preheat the oven to 350°F.

8. Remove the plastic wrap from the loaf, score it three times with a serrated knife, then bake for 45 to 60 minutes. Insert an instant-read thermometer into the center of the loaf—a reading of 350°F means it's done. Remove from the oven and allow to cool fully on a wire rack for 1 to 2 hours before slicing.

tip: Unsweetened chocolate, also known as baking chocolate, can be found in the baking aisle of the supermarket, sold in bars that can easily be broken into 1 ounce squares.

15 grams (1 tablespoon) active dry yeast

pinch of sugar

220 grams (1½ cups) all-purpose flour, plus more for dusting

220 grams (1½ cups) rye flour

90 grams (½ cup) oat bran

45 grams (¼ cup) whole-wheat flour

15 grams (2 teaspoons) salt

10 grams (1 tablespoon) caraway seeds, roughly chopped

30 grams (1 ounce) unsweetened chocolate

28 grams (2 tablespoons) vegan butter

30 grams (2 tablespoons) blackstrap molasses

20 grams (2 tablespoons) vinegar

15 grams (1 tablespoon) instant coffee granules

There is nothing like a freshly baked baguette. It's a great recipe to have in your repertoire and a bread that is fairly easy to make once you get some practice. A baguette baking sheet is a worthy investment—the shape and perforation is what helps to yield a crusty baguette. Once you've mastered the art of the baguette, you'll be able to make as many as you like in preparation for a cocktail party since they can be used with so many great appetizers and hors d'oeuvres.

baguettes

PREP TIME: 2½ HOURS

COOK TIME: 20 MINUTES

MAKES 1 BAGUETTE

pinch of sugar

7 grams (1½ teaspoons) active dry yeast

550 grams (2½ cups) bread flour, plus more for dusting

7 grams (1 teaspoon) salt

1. In a small bowl, whisk together the sugar, yeast, and 220 grams (1 cup) warm water (about 110°F). Set aside for at least 15 minutes.

2. Meanwhile, sift together the flour and salt into a large bowl.

3. Add the yeast mixture to the flour and knead into a ball, about 5 minutes. Cover with plastic wrap and set aside in a warm area to proof for 1 hour.

4. Transfer the dough to a lightly floured surface, punch down, and reform the ball about 5 times to strengthen the crust, then return to the bowl, cover again, and proof for another 30 minutes.

5. Transfer the dough back to the lightly floured surface and press the ball into a rectangular shape. Fold the right side into the center, then the left side into the center, then the top into the center, then the top to the bottom. From the center out to the sides, roll your palms back and forth on the rectangle as it works it way out to a long cylinder. Transfer the dough to a baguette baking sheet and allow to proof for an additional 30 minutes.

6. Preheat the oven to 350°F. Pour about 2 cups water into a small pan and place it in the oven to generate steam (this will help achieve a nice crust). Score the proofed dough about 5 times. Remove the water from the oven, then bake the baguette for 20 minutes. Remove from the oven and cool fully (about 1 hour) before serving.

warthog bread

PREP TIME: 2 HOURS

COOK TIME: 20 MINUTES

MAKES 1 LARGE LOAF

480 grams (3½ cups) heirloom whole-wheat flour, preferably warthog, plus more for dusting

7 grams (1 teaspoon) salt

7 grams (1½ teaspoons) active dry yeast

50 grams (¼ cup) olive oil

18 grams (1½ tablespoons) agave nectar

You've heard of heirloom tomatoes, why not heirloom wheat? Warthog is a varietal of wheat that grows here in Pennsylvania. We knead it into a delicious whole-wheat brown bread that's slightly nutty and just a touch sweet. If you can get your hands on it, fabulous. If not, ask around at your local farmers market for heirloom bread flours. Any high-protein bread flour will work well in this recipe, and you may stumble upon something really extraordinary.

1. Sift the flour, salt, and yeast into a large bowl. Add 220 grams (1 cup) cold water, the oil, and the agave, and knead until the dough forms a thick ball, about 10 minutes.

2. Dust a work surface and your hands with flour. Transfer the dough to the work surface and shape. Use your fingers to stretch the top right side of the dough ball down over the bottom left side, sealing this new seam with the palms of your hands. Repeat this fold about six times, creating a smooth ball shape, then transfer the dough back to the bowl. Cover the bowl with plastic wrap and set aside in a warm place for 45 minutes.

3. Line a sheet pan with parchment paper. Invert the dough onto the flour-dusted work surface. Dust your hands and create a small envelope by folding the right side of the dough into the center and then folding the left side into the center. Fold the top side into the center, then fold the new top side down to meet the bottom side. Now use your palms to work the new seam shut, starting in the center and working out to the two ends. You should have a rectangular loaf that you can lift off the board and onto the prepared sheet pan. Cover with plastic wrap and set aside in a warm area for an additional 30 minutes.

(RECIPE CONTINUES)

4. Preheat the oven to 400°F. Pour about 2 cups water into a small pan and place it in the oven to generate moisture while the bread bakes.

5. Remove the plastic wrap and use a serrated knife to score the loaf four times.

6. Bake for 10 minutes, rotate the sheet pan halfway, and carefully remove the pan of water. Continue baking for an additional 5 minutes.

7. Turn off the oven and leave the oven door ajar, letting the bread bake for an additional 8 minutes.

8. Remove the bread from the oven and transfer to a wire rack to cool fully, about 2 hours. Slice and serve.

cocktails

WE TREAT OUR bar like an extension of our kitchen. Our wines and beers are carefully selected based on their unique personalities and their ability to pair with a diverse range of plates. Our approach to cocktails takes this process one step further, using raw ingredients and creating our own syrups, bitters, and tinctures to customize the final drink list. The cocktails at Vedge reflect the changing seasons, showcasing interesting and sometimes hard to find spirits throughout the year. When crafting cocktails, like properly seasoning a dish, it's essential to strike the perfect balance between sweet and sour, power and finesse.

alpine sensation

PREP TIME: 5 MINUTES
SERVES 1

2 ounces cold pilsner beer, preferably Würzburger Hofbräu Premium Pilsner

1 ounce dry vermouth, preferably Dolin

1 ounce white aperitif wine, preferably Cocchi Americano

¾ ounce freshly squeezed lemon juice

1 dash (2 or 3 drops) Peychaud's bitters

Philly is a beer town, and we've offered some fun beer-based cocktails over the years. The Alpine Sensation was an instant hit. We start with a clean pilsner, just the kind you would want after a day of skiing in the Alps. (We love Würzburger Hofbräu Premium Pilsner, but feel free to use your favorite local pilsner.) We add vermouth and a little Cocchi Americano, a northern Italian specialty you will find very versatile behind your bar. Dry shaking the cocktail (without ice) helps to calm some of the carbonation in the beer, yielding a smooth texture for the drink.

1. Chill a coupe glass by filling it with ice, swirling it around, and allowing it to sit while you make the drink.

2. Combine the beer, dry vermouth, white aperitif wine, and lemon juice in a shaker. Dry shake it vigorously for 10 seconds.

3. Dump the ice out of the coupe glass and pour the shaker's contents into the chilled glass.

4. Float the dash of Peychaud's bitters on the surface and serve.

tip: Cocchi Americano can be enjoyed as an aperitif with just a spritz of seltzer water and some citrus. Dolin is our choice for vermouth in classic martinis, and Peychaud's is essential for an authentic New Orleans Sazerac, sometimes referred to as the oldest known American cocktail.

This alternative to a traditional martini playfully combines different spirits that tip the cap to the life of the famous artist (Dutch vodka, French Lillet, and a street-legal variation of his favorite hallucinogen, absinthe). It drinks really clean with just enough sweetness. The final touch, the ear-shaped clementine segment, all boozed up after soaking in the cocktail, is a juicy little garnish that pays one final tribute to the artist.

1. Chill a martini glass by filling it with ice, swirling it around, and allowing it to sit for a few minutes before dumping the ice from the glass.

2. Rinse the glass with the absinthe, discarding any that is not coating the glass.

3. Combine the vodka, dry vermouth, and lemon juice in a shaker. Fill the shaker halfway with ice and shake vigorously for 10 seconds. Strain the contents of the shaker into the glass.

4. Drop the clementine segment into the drink. Squeeze the clementine peel just above the surface of the drink to release the essential oils in the skin, then run it along the rim of the glass to impart extra flavor. Serve.

the van gogh

PREP TIME: 5 MINUTES
SERVES 1

⅛ ounce absinthe, preferably Vieux Carré

2 ounces citrus-flavored vodka, preferably Ketel One Citroen

1 ounce Lillet Blanc dry vermouth

¼ ounce freshly squeezed lemon juice

1 peeled clementine segment

One 1-inch strip clementine peel

pomegranate sangria

PREP TIME: 5 MINUTES
SERVES 1

2 ounces pomegranate juice

2 ounces red wine, preferably Tempranillo or Monastrell

½ ounce brandy

½ ounce orange liqueur, preferably Cointreau

2 tablespoons diced fresh fruit, such as grapes or oranges

If your house is anything like ours, you may find yourself with a leftover half bottle of red wine here and there. If you don't need it for cooking, consider giving it a second life in sangria. Amped up with fresh fruit from whatever season you're in, it's a delicious wine-based cocktail throughout the year. Any red wine will do, but I like Spanish wines with good acidity, and I'm partial to fresh pomegranate seeds for garnish. This recipe multiplies well, and a pitcher of sangria is a wonderful thing to have in your fridge all summer long.

1. In a shaker, combine the pomegranate juice, red wine, brandy, and orange liqueur. Stir.

2. Fill a large red wineglass halfway with ice. Add the fruit, then pour the sangria on top. Serve with a small swizzle stick or cinnamon sticks to pick the fruit.

sherry temple

PREP TIME: 5 MINUTES

SERVES 1

One ¼-inch cube peeled ginger

½ ounce freshly squeezed orange juice

2 ounces fino sherry, preferably Manzanilla

½ ounce maraschino liqueur, preferably Luxardo

½ ounce sweet vermouth, preferably Antica

1 maraschino cherry

This drink is an obvious nod to the Shirley Temple. It features Manzanilla sherry, a light, dry fino from the town of Sanlúcar de Barrameda, which lends toasty, nutty, oxidized notes to the drink. The cherry sweetness comes from both the Luxardo maraschino liqueur and their highly acclaimed authentic maraschino cherries. The liqueur is fairly easy to find, but you can substitute cherry liqueur if necessary. If you have trouble locating the cherries, any maraschino cherry will do—just try to find ones that don't use food coloring.

1. Chill a coupe glass by filling it with ice, swirling it around, and allowing it to sit while you make the drink.

2. Muddle the ginger in a shaker with the orange juice.

3. Add the sherry, maraschino liqueur, and sweet vermouth, then fill with ice and shake vigorously for 10 seconds.

4. Dump the ice out of the coupe glass and double-strain the mixer through a fine strainer over the chilled glass.

5. Garnish with the maraschino cherry and serve.

The island of Madeira changed my life. OK, I'm definitely being a little overdramatic here. But it did certainly shape my life around the time we opened Vedge. Our visit there in the summer of 2011 inspired our recipe for *Lupini* Beans with *Piri Piri* (page 41) and put Vinho Verde on the wine list. The cheesecake on Vedge's opening menu was served with Black Mission figs and "honey smacks" created with the help of the sticky fruit flavors and toasty nuttiness of Madeira wine. In addition to serving Madeira by the glass, we also developed this cocktail to help find it a broader audience. The first sip is boozy, then it turns sweet and nutty, with an appetizingly bitter finish thanks to the amaro.

1. Chill a martini glass by filling it with ice, swirling it around, and allowing it to sit while you make the drink.

2. In a shaker, combine the bourbon, Madeira, and amaro. Fill it with ice and stir for 30 seconds.

3. Dump the ice out of the martini glass and strain the shaker's contents into the chilled glass.

4. Squeeze the orange twist over the glass to release its natural oils, then drop it in the drink and serve.

the creole gent

PREP TIME: 5 MINUTES

SERVES 1

2 ounces bourbon, preferably Bulleit

1 ounce Madeira, preferably Blandy's 5-Year-Old Alvada

½ ounce amaro, preferably Cynar

1 long orange twist

I took a class years ago in an effort to develop an appreciation for sake. Prior to the class, I had never enjoyed it and couldn't understand how people could guzzle it with sushi. The most important lesson I learned was to always go for *junmai*. It's pure sake as opposed to other products that rely on the addition of distilled neutral spirits. Leaving the class, I was inspired to create a cocktail that would help turn other people on to sake. The result features the sweetness of the agave, the tartness of the grapefruit and lemon, and a garden-fresh note from the cucumber.

1. Muddle the grapefruit with the cucumber in a shaker.

2. Add the sake, agave, and lemon juice. Top with ice, then shake vigorously for 10 seconds.

3. Fill a large rocks glass halfway with ice, then double-strain the contents of the shaker through a fine strainer over the fresh ice.

4. Garnish with the grapefruit twist or cucumber slice, then serve.

tip: Watch your pronunciation. Pronounce it "sah-kee" and you're ordering salmon. "Sah-kay" is rice wine.

kyoto sour

PREP TIME: 5 MINUTES
SERVES 1

1 peeled grapefruit segment

One ½-inch slice cucumber, peeled

3 ounces junmai sake

½ ounce agave nectar

½ ounce freshly squeezed lemon juice

1 grapefruit twist or cucumber slice

the elder sage

PREP TIME: 5 MINUTES

SERVES 1

2 ounces gin, preferably Hendrick's

1 ounce elderflower liqueur, prefer-ably St-Germain

½ ounce freshly squeezed lemon juice

1 sage leaf

1 dash (2 or 3 drops) grapefruit bitters (see Tip)

We love incorporating fresh herbs and spices into our cock-tail list. Here we do a little of both, using bitters made from aromatic, dried spices and finishing the cocktail by releasing the essential oils of fresh sage on the surface of the drink. The main components of the drink are St-Germain liqueur, a beautifully aromatic spirit made from white elderflower blos-soms, and gin, full of lovely botanicals. Don't forget to slap the sage for some herbal impact!

1. Chill a coupe glass by filling it with ice, swirling it around, and allowing it to sit while you make the drink.

2. Combine the gin, elderflower liqueur, and lemon juice in a shaker. Fill the shaker halfway with ice and stir for 30 seconds.

3. Dump the ice out of the coupe glass and strain the shaker's con-tents into the chilled glass. Hold the sage leaf in one hand and apply the dash of bitters to it. Slap the sage leaf with your other hand to release its natural oils, then float it on the surface of the drink. Serve.

tip: To make your own grapefruit bitters, see page 228.

bitters

PREP TIME: 5 MINUTES

COOKTIME: 7 DAYS

MAKES 4 OUNCES

¾ cup 100-proof vodka, preferably Smirnoff

1 teaspoon angelica root, cut

½ teaspoon burdock root, cut

½ teaspoon dandelion, cut

½ teaspoon fennel seed

½ teaspoon wormwood leaves, cut

½ teaspoon rose buds, crushed

¼ teaspoon milk thistle herb, cut

1 grapefruit, washed well

Making your own bitters is surprisingly easy and allows you to customize cocktails to your personal tastes. Here we're using grapefruit to flavor the bitters for use in The Elder Sage (page 226), but you can replace the grapefruit in this recipe with anything from Meyer lemon to watermelon. Want just the tiniest hint of heat? You can create a subtle ancho-chile bitter. Want a little chocolaty note? You can make a cacao-nib bitter. It's all about infusing your neutral spirit (a high-proof vodka) and blending that with the bitter-blend in a 3 to 1 ratio. Your best bet for finding all the bitter herbs is a spice shop, but you can always order online from Penn Herb right here in Philadelphia.

1. Make the bitter-blend by combining ½ cup of the vodka with all the herbs and spices. Store in a cool, dark place for 7 days, agitating the bottle once a day.

2. On day four, slice the grapefruit into eight rings and remove any seeds. Dehydrate the grapefruit until it is entirely dry, about 3 hours in a dehydrator on the low setting or in a 200°F oven for about 45 minutes.

3. Combine the dried grapefruit with the remaining ¼ cup vodka in an airtight container. Store in a cool, dark place for at least 3 days, agitating the bottle once a day.

4. Strain the contents of both containers through a fine strainer and into a mixing bowl. Feel free to squeeze any excess vodka from the grapefruit. Pass the combined contents from the mixing bowl through a coffee filter, then transfer to an airtight bottle. Bitters will stay fresh for at least 2 months.

final note

OUR GLASSES OF Appleton rum on the rocks sweat beads of condensation in the sweet, hot, tropical night air. The salt-thick scent of the Caribbean Sea washes away any remaining grains of stress as each wave crashes on the shore.

It's dinnertime in Jamaica, and I am in heaven. The menu tonight, like every night, proudly features all the best the island has to offer: callaloo, fried breadfruit, rice n' peas, "charcoal" potato, ackee, spiced cabbage & plantains . . . It's so simple, yet so perfect. Perhaps it's the rum. Perhaps it's vacation, my mind undistracted by a million culinary tangents and finally able to focus and enjoy in a way not possible unless I'm 1,500 miles from home. Or perhaps it's because we are eating farm to table, Jamaican style. What we eat here grows here. The self-sufficiency and authenticity many of us are seeking in the US – here they've been doing it this way forever. And it's right here on the plate.

As the American dining scene evolves, so too does our awareness of our food's provenance. The American culinary experience has strayed mighty far from our original farm to table roots. While some of us rally against the grip of big agri-businesses, too many others turn a busy cheek, preoccupied by what we've convinced ourselves is important. We've been sold and fed poison masquerading as food, and it's somehow snuck its way into our supermarkets, our restaurants, and into our schools. Shame on those that put the greed of profits above health and quality, and shame on us for putting the ease of ignorance before the truth.

We can only hope that what we're doing at Vedge will help inspire people to think more about their food: where it comes from, how to prepare it, how it makes us feel. And we can only hope that this book makes it a little easier to get started or keep it going in your own home.

■ ■ ■

Another splash of rum in the glass, some coconut and mango on the plate for dessert, we're wrapping up our short time in Jamaica. The restaurant calls, as does the publisher and photographer, the contractors and consulting accounts. You can only escape life's demands for so long, but what a wonderful thing to find yourself rushing back to what you're escaped from.

Whether at the restaurant or in the pages of this book, thank you to all who have supported us over the years as customers, employees, purveyors and press. It is because of your encouragement and enthusiasm that we've been able to take this ride so far.

RSL, somewhere over the Caribbean,
February 11, 2013

acknowledgments

STARTING TO WRITE a new cookbook is very much like moving. It's easy to forget just how much work goes into it. Like taking that first picture off the wall to pack, then looking around and realizing just how much stuff you have—writing a cookbook takes a remarkable amount of time and effort. It also takes some serious help.

This cookbook was, indeed, a huge project, but we have been so lucky to work with and be surrounded by some amazingly talented people who helped us make this happen.

First thanks must go to The Experiment. Our publisher, Matthew Lore, supported our project from the start, and our editor, Cara Bedick, provided the perfect balance of half-cheerleader and half-drill sergeant we so desperately needed, and the rest of our team at the Experiment: Molly Cavanaugh, Dan O'Connor, Jack Palmer and Sarah Schneider who all helped keep this tremendous effort organized and on track. Cathy Gruhn at Hilsinger-Mendelsen East was a true pleasure to work with in getting the word out in a big way. It's not easy to tie restaurant people like us down to deadlines, but somehow, thanks to this dedicated bunch, we made it work.

We're also incredibly fortunate to have had Michael Spain-Smith on board for photography. We've worked with him on all sorts of projects over the years, but his food shots for this book are stunning and fresh. A true artist, he somehow makes the photo look more appealing that the food itself.

And big thanks to the entire Vedge staff. Our daytime prep team Allison, Katherine and Val who helped us test all the recipes showing the extra care and attention necessary for two people who normally never measure! And the rest of the Vedge staff were superstars, running the restaurant like a well-oiled machine any time we had to duck out for meetings, photo shoots, and longs sessions of editing. Daniel and Joe at the front of house and our stellar kitchen lineup: Andrew, Elpidio, Jeremy, Kelly, and Mike. Our front of the house rock stars: Ali, Bernie, Claudio, Dana, Jessica, Jessie, Joseph, Karla, Keren, Mary, Matt, Megan and Rachel. And Berfin and Gustavo for doing all the behind the scenes work that hold the place together (literally). We can't possibly overstate how much we appreciate the professionalism and talent of our entire Vedge crew.

Thanks must also go to Larry Krasner, Lisa Rau, Bob Diamond, and Jody Dodd for helping find and build our beautiful home in the Tiger building.

Our families also deserve tremendous thanks. This includes, of course, our son Rio for being pretty good about letting Daddy and Mommy focus on being authors for a while, our parents Mary Jane Jacoby and Mike & Dotsy Landau for support and encouragement as well as precious babysitting, the producers and lawyers Suzanne Landau & Rob Auritt and Rue Landau & Kerry Smith for practical advice, inspiration and love. And our amazing babysitters: Ryan Murphy, Laura & Andrew Kreider and Laura Shaeffer who helped us keep our lives in check through all the stacks of papers and extra work. Thank you all for your unconditional support and for understanding just how all-consuming the restaurant business and cookbook writing can be.

Thanks also to the wonderful media players who helped us promote this book from the very start. Joe Yonan for "getting" what we're trying to do and writing such a beautiful foreword to this book. Joseph Connelly and the team at *VegNews* for raising the hype early on. Also a sincere shout to the Philly writers and bloggers who have given us nothing but support and generous "net" time. As born and raised Philadelphians we are happy to be able to make you and our city proud. Mike Klein at Philly.com Vance Lehmkuhl at the *Philadelphia Daily News*, Jason Sheehan, Arthur Etchells and the rest of the crew at Foobooz & Philly Mag, Collin Flatt at Eater and Caroline Russock at *Philadelphia Daily City Paper*.

Best for last, our customers. From the diehard fans from the early days in Willow Grove to the guests from out of town who had just one night to check us out while they were in Philly for business last week – we are forever grateful for your support. You allow us to do what we are passionate about, and you prompt us to keep pushing, keep innovating and keep improving. We are thrilled to host you in our restaurant and happier still to make it into your home kitchens with this book, allowing us to share our vision for food and eating with an even wider audience.

Thank you for buying this book. We hope you like reading it and have fun cooking from it. Please enjoy!

index

Page references in **BOLD** indicate the main entry for the recipe; other page references indicate other uses of the recipe, a suggested pairing, or a suggested menu that includes the recipe.

about the authors

HUSBAND-WIFE TEAM Richard Landau and Kate Jacoby are the chefs/owners of Vedge.

Chef Richard Landau has been at the forefront of the vegetarian dining scene since 1994, when he opened Horizons Café in Willow Grove. His mission has been to take the carnivore palate he grew up with and use it to translate vegetarian cuisine to a broader audience. During more than five years at Horizons off South Street in Philadelphia, he continued to push the envelope of meatless cuisine. In 2009, he was invited to serve the first-ever vegan dinner at the prestigious James Beard House in Manhattan. He is proud to have helped shape the culinary landscape in Philadelphia and is excited to further raise the bar for vegetable cuisine.

Chef Kate Jacoby joined Landau in 2001 to throw her full support behind Horizons, the restaurant she had already grown to know and love as a customer. Her work on the line beside Landau helped hone her pastry skills and shaped her approach to desserts. As pastry chef, she strives to innovate vegan desserts and bring fresh ideas to rich, quality ingredients. And, as sommelier at Vedge, Kate includes the bar among her responsibilities. Her appreciation and enthusiasm for wine is evident in the lovingly selected wine list.

Landau and Jacoby are both Philadelphia natives. They spend as much of their time as possible traveling the world to find natural beauty, inspiring cultures, and exciting new foods and drinks.

about vedge

OPENED IN 2011, Vedge is a modern vegetable restaurant owned and operated by chefs Richard Landau and Kate Jacoby. Landau and Jacoby have taken their acclaimed Horizons vegan restaurant concept to the next level in Philadelphia's historic Tiger Building on Locust Street in Center City. Vedge offers a classically elegant dining experience with a progressive, bold approach to cooking.

The menus at Vedge are globally inspired, using locally sourced ingredients that closely follow the beautiful northeastern seasons. Absolutely no animal products are used in the Vedge kitchen. Behind the bar, the cocktails are fun and innovative, using house-made syrups and bitters, and the wines and beers are selected to represent the best of the boutique and craft movements.

Vedge prides itself on being a "foodie's" restaurant—for omnivores, vegetarians, and vegans alike.